**Butterworths
Capital Gains Tax
Guide**

Butterworths Capital Gains Tax Guide

Second edition

Giles Clarke
MA, PhD
of the Middle Temple, Barrister

Butterworths
London
1989

United Kingdom	Butterworth & Co (Publishers) Ltd, 88 Kingsway, LONDON WC2B 6AB and 4 Hill Street, EDINBURGH EH2 3JZ
Australia	Butterworths Pty Ltd, SYDNEY, MELBOURNE, BRISBANE, ADELAIDE, PERTH, CANBERRA and HOBART
Canada	Butterworths Canada Ltd, TORONTO and VANCOUVER
Ireland	Butterworth (Ireland) Ltd, DUBLIN
New Zealand	Butterworths of New Zealand Ltd, WELLINGTON and AUCKLAND
Puerto Rico	Equity de Puerto Rico, Inc, HATO REY
Singapore	Malayan Law Journal Pte Ltd, SINGAPORE
USA	Butterworths Legal Publishers, AUSTIN, Texas; BOSTON, Massachusetts; CLEARWATER, Florida (D & S Publishers); ORFORD, New Hampshire (Equity Publishing); ST PAUL, Minnesota; and SEATTLE, Washington

All rights reserved. No part of this publication may be reproduced or transmitted in any form or by any means (including photocopying and recording) without the written permission of the copyright holder except in accordance with the provisions of the Copyright Act 1956 (as amended) or under the terms of a licence issued by the Copyright Licensing Agency, 33-34 Alfred Place, London, England WC1E 7DP. The written permission of the copyright holder must also be obtained before any part of this publication is stored in a retrieval system of any nature. Applications for the copyright holder's written permission to reproduce, transmit or store in a retrieval system any part of this publication should be addressed to the publisher.

Warning: The doing of an unauthorised act in relation to a copyright work may result in both a civil claim for damages and criminal prosecution.

© Butterworth & Co (Publishers) Ltd 1989

A CIP Catalogue record for this book is available from the British Library.

First Edition 1988

ISBN 0 406 50550 0

Typeset by Kerrypress Ltd, Luton
Printed and bound in Great Britain by Mackays of Chatham plc, Kent

Preface

In this book, I have described Capital Gains Tax as it exists after the 1989 Finance Act. I hope this book will be useful both to those new to the subject and to those whose knowledge requires updating.

The book could not have been written without the help of my wife, Deborah Morris, my clerk, Sarah Frampton, and her assistants, Marie Tucker and Elaine Graves. To all of them I am grateful. I should also record that some of the examples are derived from *Sumption's Capital Gains Tax*, where they were prepared by John Risby and his colleagues at Arthur Andersen & Co.

The law is stated as at 1 August 1989.

Verulam Buildings   Giles Clarke
Gray's Inn   *1 August 1989*
London

*For
Deborah*

Contents

Preface v
Table of statutes ix
List of cases xiii

I. General Principles 1
   1 Gains and losses 3
   2 Assets 6
   3 Disposals 10
   4 Market value and connected persons 17

II. Computation 21
   5 Consideration 23
   6 Allowable expenditure 28
   7 Pooling and identification 35
   8 1982 rebasing 40
   9 Indexation 49

III. Chargeable Entities 57
   10 Individuals 59
   11 Companies 64
   12 Trusts and settlements 70

IV. Exemptions 77
   13 Private residences 79
   14 Exempt intangibles 86
   15 Exempt chattels 92
   16 Retirement relief 95
   17 Death 101

V. Deferrals 105
   18 Hold-over relief 107
   19 Replacement of business assets 113
   20 Other roll-over reliefs 120
   21 Reorganisations, mergers and reconstructions 124

Contents

VI. Foreign Element 131
    22   Territorial limits   133
    23   Shareholders in non-resident companies   139
    24   Beneficiaries under non-resident trusts   142

VII. Tax Planning 147
    25   Personal planning   149
    26   Business planning   156
    27   Capital and income   164

Index 171

Table of Statutes

	PAGE
Capital Gains Tax Act 1979	3, 4, 49
s 2	59
4	61
5	59
7A	112
10	137
12	134
13	136
14	136
15	139
(5), (7)	140
16	141
18	133
(4)(j)	136
19	6
(2)	11
(5)	88
20	12, 13
21	122
22	14
23(3)	23
25	14
26	24
27	11
29	4
29A	17, 24, 65, 74
(1)(b)	23
31	24
32	28
(1)(a)	28
(b)	29
(2)	29
32A	168
33, 34	30
35	31
36	28
37	8, 32
38	32
39	32

	PAGE
Capital Gains Tax Act 1979—*contd*	
s 40	25
41	25
43	28
44, 45	61
46	70
47	102
49	102
(1)–(3)	101
(4)	102
52	71, 133, 134
53–56	72
58	74
(2)	74
60	62
62, 63	18
65	36
66	37
67	86
72	65
78–81	124, 125
82	39, 86, 126
(3)(b)	126
83	126
85	124, 126
86	127
87	128
88	128
92	69
93	69
101	79
(2)–(4)	83
(5)	82
102	80
(4)	82
103	83
(3)	85
104	84

Table of Statutes

	PAGE
Capital Gains Tax Act 1979—	
contd	
s 105	84
107	31
111A	121
115	113, 115, 116
(6)	115
116, 117	113, 117
118	113, 114
119	113
120	113, 118
121	113
123	120
124	95
126	107, 108, 109, 110, 111, 112, 152
(3)–(6), (9), (10)	110
126A	107
(2)	138
126B	107
(2)	138
126C	111
(9)	138
127	93
128	92
130, 131	93
133	88, 93
134	87
135	88
136	87
137	27
138	9
144A	169
147A	107, 109, 110, 111, 112
(3)–(9)	110
147B	109
(2)	138
149C	89
(4)	90
149D	90
150	17
155	101
Sch 1	72
para 4	102
6	72
Sch 2	86
Sch 3	7, 26
para 1	9, 33
2	25
Sch 4	107
para 1	109
2	108

	PAGE
Capital Gains Tax Act 1979—	
contd	
Sch 5	40
para 11	52
Companies Act 1985	
s 162	167
427	127
Finance Act 1980	
s 79	107
80	82
81	69
117	129
Sch 17 para 9	129
Sch 18	129
Finance Act 1981	
s 79	111
80	142, 143
82	145
83	144
(6)	142
85	141
88	146
Finance Act 1982	
s 86	41, 49
87	49, 50
(3)(a)	55
88	36, 38
Sch 13	52
para 5	125
8, 9	38
Finance Act 1984	
s 50	113
64	86, 125
(7)	87
Sch 11	113
Sch 13	125
Finance Act 1985	
s 68	44, 49
(4)	51
(7)	52, 67
(9)	37
69	95, 97, 98
(1)	95
(4)	98
70	95
(1), (3)	100
(5)	99
71	18
Sch 19	36
para 6, 7	38
8–10	37
11–14	53
18	37, 55

Table of Statutes

	PAGE
Finance Act 1985—*contd*	
Sch 20	95, 96
para 1	98, 99
3	95
4	96
6	100
8	99
10	100
12	97
13–16	96
Finance Act 1986	
s 58	138
Finance Act 1988	
s 50, 51	89
66	133
96	5, 38, 40
(3)	41, 44
(5)	41
98	60
99	61
(4)	62
100	73
104	60
105	135
106	138
107	135
111	84
112	114
113	55
118	52
Sch 7	134
Sch 8 para 1	41, 44, 67
2	67
8	79
9	115
10	41
13	41, 67
14	67
Sch 9	45, 47, 48, 118, 123, 157
Sch 10	73
Sch 11	68
Finance Act 1989	48
s 105	65
123	92
124	107
126–131	134
132	134, 138
133, 134	134
138	66
139(3), (5)	87
Sch 15	
para 1	48

	PAGE
Finance (No 2) Act 1975	
s 58	37
Financial Services Act 1986 . .	69
s 78	69
Income and Corporation Taxes Act 1970	
s 267	128, 129
272	66
273	68
276	118
(1)	118
278	66, 67
280, 281	68
482	135
Income and Corporation Taxes Act 1988	
s 6	64
11	134
13	64, 65
13A	65
14	65
34	27
65(6)–(8)	136
75	156
135	168
188(3)	188
208	68
213–218	129
219, 225, 239	167
287	61
335	133
345	64, 65
356	80
383	156
414, 415	139
416	19
468	69
469(7)	69
672–674, 677	74
686	73
710	39
757–764	39
790	137
796, 797	137
832, 838	66
Sch 4	39
Sch 9	168
Sch 18	86
Inheritance Tax Act 1984	
s 2(3)	110
3A	109, 154
71(4)	109
105(1)(d)	158

Table of Statutes

	PAGE
Inheritance Tax Act 1984—*contd*	
s 116	109
142	103
267	136

	PAGE
Insolvency Act 1986	
s 110	127, 160
Landlord and Tenant Act 1954:	8
Trustee Act 1925	
s 37(1)(c)	151

List of Cases

A

Aberdeen Construction Group Ltd v IRC (1978) 4, 29, 87
Allison v Murray (1975) . . . 29
Atkinson v Dancer (1988) . . 98

B

Batey v Wakefield (1981) . . . 79
Bayley v Rogers (1980) 8, 29
Berry v Warnett (1982) 10
Bond v Pickford (1983) . . . 71, 72
Booth v Ellard (1978) 70
Brumby v Milner (1976) . . . 168

C

Chaney v Watkis (1986) . . . 29
Cleveleys Investment Trust v IRC (1975) 28
Craven v White (1988): 5, 11, 154, 163

D

Davenport v Chilver (1983) . . 7, 13
De Beers Consolidated Mines Ltd v Howe (1906) . . . 133
Dunstan v Young, Austen and Young Ltd (1987); revsd (1989) 125, 126

E

Eastham v Leigh London and Provincial Properties Ltd (1971) 11

F

Floor v Davis (1978) 10, 14
Floor v Davis (1980) 128
Frost v Feltham (1981) 80
Furniss v Dawson (1984) . 5, 10, 128

I

IRC v Buchanan (1914) . . . 17
IRC v Burmah Oil Co Ltd (1982) 4
IRC v Clay (1914) 17
IRC v Richards' Executors (1971) 28, 29, 102
IRC v Matthews' Executors (1984) 101

J

Jenkins v Brown (1989) . . . 63

K

Kidson v Macdonald (1974) . . 71
Kirby v Thorn EMI plc (1987) 7, 10, 13

L

Law Shipping Co Ltd v IRC (1923) 30

M

McGregor v Adcock (1977) . . 98
Makins v Elson (1977) 79
Markey v Sanders (1987) . . . 79
Marren v Ingles (1980) . . 6, 12, 23, 127

List of Cases

	PAGE
Marson v Marriage (1980)	13, 23, 25, 26
Moore v Thompson (1986)	79

O

O'Brien v Benson's Hosiery (Holdings) Ltd (1979)	6, 13
Owen v Elliott (1989)	82

P

Passant v Jackson (1986)	29
Pennine Raceway Ltd v Kirklees Metropolitan Council (No 2) (1989)	13

R

R v IRC, ex p Fulford-Dobson (1987)	59
Ramsay (WT) Ltd v IRC (1982)	4, 10, 87
Rank Xerox Ltd v Lane (1979)	6
Reed v Clark (1985)	149
Roome v Edwards (1981)	71, 72

S

Simmons v IRC (1980)	164
South African Supply and Cold Storage Co, Re (1904)	127
Stamp Duties Comr v Livingstone (1964)	101

	PAGE
Stephenson v Barclays Bank Trust Co Ltd (1975)	71

T

Temperley v Visibell Ltd (1964)	114
Todd v Mudd (1987)	114
Tomlinson v Glyns Executor and Trustee Co (1970)	71

U

Unit Construction Co Ltd v Bullock (1960)	133

V

Varty v Lynes (1976)	83, 84

W

Welbeck Securities Ltd v Powlson (1987)	10
Whitehead's Will Trusts, Re (1971)	151
Williams v Bullivant (1983)	14
Williams v Evans (1982)	114
Williams v Merrylees (1987)	79

Z

Zim Properties Ltd v Procter (1985)	6, 13, 88

I General Principles

Chapter 1

Gains and Losses

Introduction

Capital Gains Tax is a tax on the chargeable gains which accrue on the disposal of assets. It is not assessed as and when a particular asset is disposed of, but instead the charge is on the balance of chargeable gains accruing in a year of assessment, credit being given for allowable losses.

Capital Gains Tax is payable by individuals and trusts. In each year of assessment a computation is made of the taxpayer's taxable amount. This is the aggregate of his chargeable gains, as reduced by allowable losses (see p 59). A basic annual exemption is then allowed, and the resultant net figure is charged at the taxpayer's marginal rate of income tax (see pp 60 and 73).

Companies do not pay Capital Gains Tax as such. Instead their chargeable gains are included in the profits for the accounting period concerned, and are subject to Corporation Tax (see p 64). The gains so included are computed in the same way as for Capital Gains Tax, and they are reduced by any allowable losses.

Chargeable gains

The computation of a chargeable gain involves three stages. First, the unindexed gain or loss has to be computed in accordance with rules set out in CGTA 1979, Part II, Chapter II. Then the indexation allowance is applied, to give what is called the gain for the purposes of CGTA 1979. Thirdly, any applicable exempting and relieving provisions are applied, and what is left is the chargeable gain.

The computational rules in CGTA 1979 neither define the term 'gain' in general terms, not quantify it. Instead the legislation includes a series of specific rules relating to consideration (see chapter 5) and a further series of rules relating to which expenditure is allowable (see chapter 6). One is left to infer that in general, unindexed gains are computed in the same way as trading profits, namely by deducting allowable expenditure from the proceeds of the disposal.

The fact that the term 'gain' is not defined is significant, for it means that in situations not covered by specific legislative rules, it is a question of fact as to whether and to what extent an unindexed gain has accrued. This was recognised by the House of Lords in *Aberdeen Construction Group Ltd v IRC* [1978] STC 127, where Lord Wilberforce observed that the purpose of the tax 'is to tax capital gains' which 'ought to be arrived at on normal business principles'. In a much quoted dictum, he said that 'capital gains tax is a tax on gains; it is not a tax on arithmetical differences'. This dictum, and the approach implicit in it, was approved in *W T Ramsay Ltd v IRC* [1982] AC 300, where Lord Wilberforce made the further observation that the courts are entitled to disregard a gain 'which appears to arise at one stage in an indivisible process and which is intended to be and is cancelled out by a later stage'.

Allowable losses (CGTA 1979 s.29)

It is fundamental to the scheme of CGT that allowable losses may be set against chargeable gains. A loss is allowable if, had the disposal thrown up a gain, that gain would have been chargeable. Accordingly, any provision which exempts a gain from chargeability applies equally to disallow any loss. One result of this is that some apparently relieving provisions do not give relief at all, for they apply to assets which are almost invariably disposed of at a loss.

Allowable losses are computed in the same way as chargeable gains. Thus the first stage is to compute the loss or gain in accordance with CGTA 1979 Part II, Chapter II. Then the indexation allowance is applied, and this will either increase the loss, or, because it exceeds an unindexed gain, turn a gain into a loss. That loss is known as the loss for the purposes of CGTA 1979. The final stage is to apply the exempting and relieving provisions, to the effect that the loss is allowable if, had the disposal resulted in a gain, that gain would have been chargeable.

In *IRC v Burmah Oil Co Ltd* [1982] STC 30 the House of Lords held that even if a loss is allowable on a literal reading of the legislation it is not allowable unless it is 'a loss such as the legislation is dealing with' or in short 'a real loss'. The House of Lords arrived at this conclusion by applying the dicta of Lord Wilberforce in the *Aberdeen Construction* case and in *Ramsay*, noted above. A loss is only disallowed in this way if the disposals generating the loss have no commercial purpose other than the creation of the allowable loss, and they form part of a series of transactions which can properly be described as preordained (*Furniss v Dawson* [1984] AC 474). A series of transactions is preordained if there is no practical likelihood they will not all be carried through when the first is entered into (*Craven v White* [1988] STC 476).

If the taxpayer's allowable losses exceed his chargeable gains for a year of assessment, the excess may be carried forward and set against chargeable gains in future years. Allowable losses may not be carried back, save insofar as incurred in the year of assessment in which the taxpayer dies (see p 101). Companies cannot set any net losses in an accounting period against income profits, although net gains may be offset by trading losses (see p 64).

1982 rebasing

CGT was first enacted in 1965, and it was fundamental to the tax that gains accruing before 6 April 1965 would not be chargeable. Two methods gave effect to this, namely exempting a proportionate part of gains on a straight-line basis, and deeming assets to be disposed of and reacquired at their market value on 6 April 1965.

In 1988 the base date for CGT was brought forward to 31 March 1982 (FA 1988 s.96). The basic rule is that all assets acquired before then are deemed to have been reacquired at market value on that date. There is no straight-line apportionment but, in certain circumstances, actual acquistion cost can still apply (see p 41).

Capital and income

Although Capital Gains Tax is called Capital Gains Tax, it is not in terms restricted to capital gains. Instead, this result is achieved in a roundabout way. On the one hand, receipts chargeable to income tax or included in a trading computation are excluded, and on the other, expenditure allowable in an income tax computation is disallowed (see pp 24 and 30).

Chapter 2
Assets

Introduction (CGTA 1979 s.19)

A gain or loss does not accrue unless an asset has been disposed of. All forms of property are assets for CGT purposes and this means that the term extends to any rights which the taxpayer can turn to account. It matters not that the rights cannot be transferred or assigned or that they would not vest in a trustee in bankruptcy (*O'Brien v Benson's Hosiery (Holdings) Ltd* [1979] STC 735).

Specific assets (CGTA 1979 s.19)

Certain forms of property are specifically designated as assets. They include the following:

(a) options
(b) debts
(c) incorporeal property generally
(d) foreign currency
(e) property created by the taxpayer.

The courts have given the term 'asset' a wide construction and decided that it includes the following:

(1) the employer's rights under a service agreement (*O'Brien v Benson's Hosiery (Holdings) Ltd* [1979] STC 735);
(2) a contractual right to annual payments (*Rank Xerox Ltd v Lane* [1979] STC 740);
(3) a right to additional consideration where both the right and the amount are contingent on the happening of certain events (*Marren v Ingles* [1980] STC 500);
(4) a right of action (*Zim Properties Ltd v Procter* [1985] STC 90);

(5) a right to compensation under a foreign compensation order (*Davenport v Chilver* [1983] STC 426);
(6) goodwill (*Kirby v Thorn EMI plc* [1987] STC 621).

So far the only limitation placed on the term 'asset' is that it does not include mere hopes or non proprietary rights. Thus the possibility of benefitting under a living person's will is not an asset and nor is the hope of obtaining ex gratia compensation (*Davenport v Chilver* [1983] STC 426). So too, public rights and freedoms such as the freedom to trade do not count as assets (*Kirby v Thorn EMI plc* [1987] STC 621).

Assets and interests in assets.

Since the term 'asset' includes all forms of property which can be turned to account, interests in assets are assets in their own right. Thus land is an asset, and so too is any lease, easement or option. It is not wholly clear how the doctrine of estates applies to CGT, but the better view is that a freeholder simply owns freehold land.

Beneficial interests in trusts are assets just as much as the trust property, although in practice most beneficial interests are exempt (see p 74). If the trustee is purely a nominee the property concerned is treated as directly owned by the beneficiary. Shares in a company are assets separate from property owned by the company and so too are units in authorised Unit Trusts (see p 69). Partners, by contrast, are treated as owning a fractional share in each partnership asset rather than a partnership interest (see p 62).

Unidentifiable assets

Many assets cannot be individually identified. The most obvious example are shares of the same class, but commodities and securities also exhibit this feature. Should a taxpayer own several such assets in the same class, it is impossible to identify a particular acquisition with a particular disposal. This poses problems for a tax such as CGT, taxing as it does the difference between the acquisition cost and the proceeds of disposal.

Over the years Parliament has adopted two solutions to this problem. The first is pooling, whereby all assets in a given class or category are treated as a single asset, which grows or diminishes according to whether individual assets are acquired or sold.

Assets

The second is rules of identification, whereby disposals are arbitrarily identified with acquisitions either on a last-in first-out basis or on a first-in last-out basis. The present position is that pooling is now the general rule, rules of identification applying only to what are termed 'relevant securities' (see chapter 7).

Temporal and spatial difficulties

It is sometimes difficult to tell whether a piece of property is one large asset or several small ones. Most obviously this arises with land, where the issue may be whether an estate is a single asset or several assets represented by its component parts. The legislation gives no guidance but Revenue practice regarding land has been published (BTR [1969] 438). Basically, a single acquisition of land is treated as a single asset unless on the facts it is obvious that more than one asset is involved.

Difficulties can also arise in distinguishing assets in time. Thus in *Bayley v Rogers* [1980] STC 544, a new business lease granted pursuant to the provisions of the Landlord and Tenant Act 1954 was held to be a different asset from the old lease. In some cases, identifying assets temporally is of little practical importance, for if one asset is derived from another in the same ownership, expenditure on the old asset can be carried forward to the new (see p 28).

In certain instances, two obviously distinct assets are treated as the same asset for CGT purposes. The best-known examples occur on company reorganisations and reconstructions and on takeovers involving a share for share exchange. Here, the shares held by the shareholder after the transaction are treated as the same asset as the shares he held before (see chapter 21).

Wasting assets (CGTA 1979 s.37)

Some assets have an inherently short life. This presents difficulties for a tax based on gains and losses, for of neccessity such assets will normally be disposed of at a loss. The CGT legislation overcomes this difficulty by the concept of the wasting asset. A wasting asset is an asset whose predictable life is 50 years or less, and the basic rule is that expenditure on it is written off over its predicted life (see p 32).

Wasting assets include plant and machinery, leases and options. Any plant and machinery is ipso facto treated as a wasting

Exempt assets

asset, for its predictable life is conclusively presumed to be less than 50 years. Leases granted for a term of less than 50 years are necessarily wasting assets, and leases granted for a longer term become wasting assets once the unexpired residue falls below 50 years (CGTA 1979 Sch 3 para 1). The life of an option ends when the time for exercise expires, but certain options are not treated as wasting assets, notably quoted, traded, and financial options and options to acquire trading stock (CGTA 1979 s.138).

Exempt assets

Certain assets are outside the ambit of CGT, in the sense that gains or losses accruing on their disposal are neither chargable nor allowable. Most of the assets concerned are discussed more fully later in this work and they include the following:-

1. the taxpayer's only or main residence, and its garden up to a limit of one acre, or more in certain cases (chapter 13);
2. gilt-edged securities (see p 86);
3. qualifying corporate bonds (see p 86);
4. chattles worth less than £6,000 (see p 92);
5. private cars (see p 93);
6. tangible movable assets which are wasting assets and not used for business purposes (see p 93);
7. foreign currency for personal expenditure and foreign bank accounts representing such currency (see pp 88 and 93);
8. simple debts, so long as owned by the original creditor (see p 87);
9. beneficial interests owned by the original beneficiary under a resident settlement (see p 74);
10. shares granted BES relief which has not been withdrawn (see p 89);
11. investments held in a Personal Equity Plan (see p 90).

Chapter 3

Disposals

Actual disposals

A disposal must be identified before a gain or loss can accrue. In many circumstances, a disposal is deemed to take place for CGT purposes but otherwise the term 'disposal' is not defined. Essentially it envisages the transfer of ownership of an asset by one person to another or the transfer of the beneficial title to property by one person in favour of another (*Kirby v Thorn EMI plc* [1987] STC 621; *Welbeck Securities Ltd v Powlson* [1987] STC 468).

The courts have repeatedly emphasised that 'disposal' is not a term of art. Thus Lord Wilberforce has observed that there is 'no limitation on the generality of the word "disposal", which must be taken to bear its normal meaning' (*Berry v Warnett* [1982] STC 396 at 399). In *Floor v Davis,* Eveleigh LJ commented that 'there is no legal definition of the word disposal and I can see no reason to define it as the first legal transfer in the ownership of property' (see [1978] STC 436,445). Eveleigh LJ's judgement in *Floor v Davis* was a dissenting judgement, but it was subsequently approved by the House of Lords in *W T Ramsay Ltd v IRC* [1982] AC 300.

Floor v Davis and subsequent House of Lords decisions also establish that what would otherwise be a series of separate disposals may be taxed as a single disposal. Thus in *Furniss v Dawson* [1984] AC 474, an exchange by shareholders of shares in company A for shares in company B, followed on the same day by a sale by company B of the shares in company A to the ultimate purchaser, was treated as a single disposal to that purchaser by the original shareholders. But separate disposals are only so treated if they have no commercial purpose apart from the avoidance of tax, and form part of a preordained series of transactions (*Furniss v Dawson* [1984] AC 474). A series of transactions is only preordained if there is no practical likelihood they will not all be carried through when the first is entered into (*Craven v White* [1988] STC 476).

Part disposals (CGTA 1979 s.19(2))

Part disposals count as disposals. A part disposal occurs where a right or interest is created over the asset or where part of the asset is retained after the disposal. Obvious examples include the grant of a lease or the sale of part of a field.

Time of disposal (CGTA 1979 s.27)

The actual time at which a disposal takes place may be perfectly clear, as, for instance, where ownership passes on delivery. Where, as is usually the case with real property and shares, the disposal is under a contract, the date of the contract is the date of disposal. But if the contract is conditional, and in particular if it is conditional on the exercise of an option, the date of disposal is the date when the condition is satisfied or the option is exercised.

A conditional contract for these purposes is one subject to a contingent condition precedent to performance. This is a condition which neither party covenants to bring about but which has to be satisfied before liability to perform the contract arises. It is to be distinguished from a promissory condition precedent to performance (*Eastham* v *Leigh London and Provincial Properties Ltd* [1971] Ch 871). This forms part of the consideration given by one of the parties, and it is only precedent in the sense that its performance is precedent to the performance of other terms of the contract.

The distinction is illustrated by *Eastham v Leigh London and Provincial Properties Ltd* [1971] Ch 871, where the taxpayer had covenanted to erect an office block and, if the office block was completed to its satisfaction, the freeholder undertook to grant the taxpayer a long lease. Since the covenant to erect the office block was part of the consideration which the taxpayer gave for the lease, it was a promissory condition precedent to performance, and the contract was not conditional. The acquisition of the lease, therefore, took place when the contract was concluded and not when the offices were completed. The position would have been otherwise if there had been no obligation on the taxpayer to build the offices, for then the condition would have been a contingent condition precedent.

Disposals

Deemed disposals

In certain instances a disposal is deemed to take place even if the asset remains in the ownership of the taxpayer. In most cases, the intention is to trigger a charge to tax where one would not otherwise fall due. But in certain instances the deemed disposal can crystalise an allowable loss and so operates as a relieving provision.

Three kinds of deemed disposal are described below. Other events which trigger a deemed disposal include the following:

(1) The occasion on which a beneficiary becomes absolutely entitled to settled property (p 72);
(2) the receipt of a capital distribution from a company (p 65);
(3) the occasion on which a company leaves a group if and insofar as it has acquired assets within the preceding six years from other group members. This deemed disposal is backdated to the time of its acquisition of the assets concerned (see p 67);
(4) the occasion on which qualifying investments are withdrawn in specie from a mature Personal Equity Plan (p 91).

Capital sums derived from assets (CGTA 1979 s.20)

Section 20 of the Capital Gains Tax Act deems a disposal to take place when any capital sum is derived from an asset. This rule mostly renders the question of whether an actual disposal has occurred academic. The date on which the disposal occurs is the date on which the capital sum is received.

Section 20 is expressed as applying in particular to certain kinds of capital sum. They are as follows:

(a) compensation for damage or injury to an asset, for the loss, destruction or dissipation of the asset, or for the depreciation of the asset;
(b) insurance monies;
(c) sums received in return for the forfeiture or surrender of rights or for not exercising them;
(d) sums received as consideration for the use or exploitation of assets.

Case law provides the following illustrations of the application of s.20:

(1) In *Marren v Ingles* [1980] STC 500, the taxpayer sold shares for a consideration consisting of an immediate cash sum and a conditional and unquantified amount payable at

Capital sums derived from assets (CGTA 1979 s.20)

a future date. Both the right to receive the latter amount, and its quantification depended on future profits of the company whose shares were sold. It was held that the contingent right was an asset, and that the payment eventually made in satsfaction of it was a capital sum derived from it.

(2) In *Marson v Marriage* [1980] STC 177, land was sold for an immediate cash sum and a right to future payment dependant on planning permission and compulsory acquisition. Here the payment eventually made in satisfaction of the contingent right was a capital sum derived from it.

(3) In *O'Brien v Benson's Hosiery (Holdings) Ltd* [1979] STC 735, the taxpayer company had engaged a valued employee under a seven-year service contract. Subsequently it agreed to release the employee in consideration of a payment of £50,000. This sum was within s.20, for it was received in return for the surrender of the taxpayer's rights under the service contract or for refraining from exercising them.

(4) In *Davenport v Chilver* [1983] STC 426, Latvian assets belonging to the taxpayer's family has been expropriated by the Russians in 1940. In 1968 the British and Russian governments agreed to compensation being made out of Latvian assets frozen in the United Kingdom, and these arrangements were enshrined in a Foreign Compensation Order. Here the order was an asset, from which the compensation paid was derived.

(5) In *Zim Properties v Proctor* [1985] STC 90, a right of action was held to be an asset, from which sums paid to compromise the action were derived.

(6) In *Kirby v Thorn EMI plc* [1987] STC 621, a covenant was given by the ultimate parent in a large group when another group member disposed of three operating subsidiaries. The covenant was that no present or future member of the group would engage in business competing with that of the operating companies being sold. The Court of Appeal decided (i) the ultimate parent possessed goodwill in respect of the trades of the three operating subsidiaries, (ii) that goodwill, like any other goodwill, is an asset, and accordingly, (iii) the sum paid for the covenant was derived from this asset.

(7) In *Pennine Raceway Ltd v Kirklees Metropolitan Council (No 2)* [1989] STC 122 the taxpayer owned a licence to use land for drag racing, for which planning permission had been granted. The Local Authority revoked the

Disposals

planning permission and had to compensate the taxpayer. The Court of Appeal held that the compensation was within s.20 for it was compensation for depreciation of the taxpayer's licence to use the land.

Value shifting (CGTA 1979 s.25)

Certain kinds of value shifting occasion a deemed disposal at market value. They are as follows:

(1) Persons who control a company are deemed to dispose of their shares if they exercise control to pass value out of their shares and into other shares.
(2) A lessee is deemed to dispose of an interest in his lease if the lease was acquired on a sale and leaseback and it is varied in favour of the lessor.
(3) A right or restriction over an asset is deemed to be disposed of if it is extinguished or abrogated.

An example of value shifting in relation to shares occurred in *Floor v Davies* [1978] STC 379. In that case preferred and ordinary shares carried equal voting rights, but the ordinary shares were entitled to virtually all the assets on a liquidation. The ordinary shares were held by a tax-haven entity but the taxpayers controlled the company by virtue of a holding of preference shares. The House of Lords held that the passing of a resolution to wind up the company was a value shifting transaction, triggering a deemed disposal by the taxpayers of their preference shares.

Lost and valueless assets (CGTA 1979 s.22)

The occasion of the entire loss, destruction, dissipation or extinction of an asset constitutes a disposal. It is to be emphasised that this is a relieving, not a charging provision, for it enables an allowable loss to be established.

Assets whose value has become negligible may also be treated as disposed of. But this only happens if the taxpayer makes a claim to the Inspector, specifying the value to which the asset is reduced. If the Inspector is satisfied as to the claim, he is empowered to allow it, and 'thereupon' the deemed disposal takes place. The word 'thereupon' indicates that strictly the deemed disposal does not take place until the claim is allowed, although the Revenue construe it as backdating the deemed disposal to the date of the claim (*Williams v Bullivant* [1983] STC 107).

Exempt disposals and deferrals

By concession the taxpayer may treat the deemed disposal as having taken place in an earlier year provided: (i) the asset is of negligible value both then and when the claim is made; and (ii) the claim is made within two years of the year concerned (ESC 27 July 1988).

For the purposes of these rules a building is regarded as an asset separate from the land on which it stands. This enables taxpayers to elect for a deemed disposal when a building is destroyed or becomes valueless. But the value of the land still has to be brought into account, for it is deemed to be disposed of at the same time as the building.

Exempt disposals and deferrals

The CGT legislation provides for four main kinds of exemption or deferral:

(1) Outright exemption, whereby a disposal is relieved without affecting other assets of the disponor or the recipient's acquisition cost.
(2) No gain/no loss disposals. In these cases the asset is treated as passing at the disponor's acquistion cost, with the result that any gain or loss which would otherwise have accrued to him is passed on to the recipient.
(3) Hold-over relief. Here the disposal takes place at full value, but the disponor is not charged on the gain and it is deducted from the acquisition cost of the person acquiring the asset.
(4) Roll-over relief. Here too the disponor avoids an immediate charge, but the gain is deducted from the acquisition cost of assets he acquires in replacement.

The principal outright exemptions are as follows:

(1) the basic annual exemption (p 59);
(2) death (chapter 17);
(3) retirement relief (chapter 16);
(4) disposals by non-residents (chapter 22);
(5) disposals of exempt assets such as are listed on p 9;

The following are principal instances of no loss/no gain disposals:

(1) disposals between spouses living together (p 61);

Disposals

(2) disposals between member companies of a group subject to the recipient remaining in the group for at least six years (p 66);
(3) disposals between companies involved in a bona fide reconstruction or amalgamation (p 127).

Hold-over relief applies to the following gifts and similar transactions if the parties so elect:

(1) gifts of business assets (see p 107);
(2) gifts to discretionary trusts (see p 109);
(3) occasions on which a beneficiary becomes absolutely entitled to certain business assets or to assets held in an accumulation and maintenance trust (see pp 108 and 109);
(4) gifts and similar transactions involving heritage property (see p 110).

Roll-over relief applies in the following circumstances:

(1) on the disposal and replacement of business assets if the taxpayer so claims (chapter 19);
(2) on the transfer of a business to a company in exchange for shares (p 120);
(3) on the receipt of insurance or compensation monies which are applied in replacing the lost asset (p 122);
(4) on the receipt of compulsory purchase compensation which is applied in buying new land (p 121).

Chapter 4

Market Value and Connected Persons

Substitution of market value (CGTA 1979 s.29A)

On many disposals and acquisitions, the market value of the asset is substituted for the actual consideration (if any) agreed between the parties. The main circumstances in which this happens is if the transaction is not a bargain at arm's length. In particular, market value is substituted on gifts, on the transfer of assets into a settlement, and on the distribution in specie of assets by a company. Market value is also substituted where the actual consideration cannot be valued or where it consists of services to be rendered by the person acquiring the asset.

Market value is not substituted on an acquisition if there is no corresponding disposal, and either there is no actual consideration or it is less than market value. This restriction was introduced in 1981, to counter schemes which artificially inflated the base cost of blocks on shares by means of a rights issue at par. Its effect is, however, wider, and it means inter alia that in law a right of action has no acquisition cost, for the defendant has made no disposal to the plaintiff (see p 88). It also means that an original beneficiary under a settlement has no acquisition cost, for the settlor makes a disposal not to him but to the trustees (see p 74).

Determining market value (CGTA 1979 s.150)

The market value of an asset is the price which it might reasonably be expected to fetch on a sale in the open market. Account must be taken of special purchasers ie persons who would be prepared to pay a special price (*IRC v Clay and Buchanan* [1914] 3 KB 466). If several assets are being valued and their price would be depressed if they were sold at the same time, no reduction is made to take account of this.

Market value and connected persons

Quoted shares and securities are valued in accordance with the Stock Exchange Daily Official List. Unless special circumstances obtain, shares are valued at the lower of:

(a) the lower price shown in the Daily List plus one quarter of the difference between that price and the higher price; or
(b) half-way between the lowest and highest price at which bargains were recorded on the day concerned.

Unquoted shares are valued in what can only be called a hypothetical open market. In practice, a figure is arrived at by negotiation between the taxpayer's advisers and the Share Valuation Division of the Inland Revenue. The hypothetical purchaser is assumed to have all the information which a prudent purchaser might reasonably require.

The market value of assets disposed of to connected persons in a series of transactions may be a fraction of their aggregate value if that value is higher than the sum of their individual values (FA1985 s.71). This only applies if the transactions are linked, which in broad terms means the transactions must take place within six years of each other.

Connected persons (CGTA 1979 ss.62 and 63)

A transaction between connected person is ipso facto treated as a bargain not at arm's length. This means market value is substituted regardless of whether the parties have in fact conducted a proper negotiation or been independently advised.

Connected persons have a significance to CGT far beyond the market value rule. The categories of connected person are as follows:

(1) individuals are connected if they are spouses, relatives or spouses of relatives. Relatives comprise ancestors and descendants and brothers and sisters;
(2) the trustees and settlor of a settlement are connected, as are the trustees and any person connected with the settlor;
(3) partners are connected with each other and with each other's relatives;
(4) companies are connected if they are under common control;
(5) a company and any person who controls it are connected.

Persons not connected

Although these catergories are wide, certain relationships fall outside them. Well-known examples include the following:
  (a) Individuals are not connected with uncles, nephews and cousins.
  (b) Trustees are not connected with beneficiaries. In many cases, this is academic, for if the beneficiaries are connected with the settlor, that connection extends to the trustees. But any such connection ceases once the settlor is dead, and as a result, once the settlor is dead, trustees can never be connected with beneficiaries.
  (c) Partners are not connected in relation to acquisitions or disposals of partnership assets pursuant to bona fide commercial transactions. Unfortunately this is not as wide as it seems, for it does not prevent partners being connected if they are spouses or relatives.

Company connections

Connections involving companies are particularly wide-ranging. This is principally for the following reasons:
  (a) A person has control of a company if he has control within the meaning of TA 1988 s.416. Control for these purposes basically means a majority of votes in general meeting but it also includes the right to half of any dividend or the right to half of the company's assets on a liquidation.
  (b) Companies count as under common control if they are controlled by a person and persons connected with him, and similarly a person controls a company if he and persons connected with him control it.
  (c) Companies also count as under common control if a group of people control each, and the groups consist either of the same persons or persons connected with them.

These difficulties are compounded by a further rule which provides that persons are treated as connected if they act together to secure or exercise control of a company. They are only so treated in relation to the company concerned, but otherwise this rule is of the widest application, for it effectively means that almost every unquoted company is connected with its shareholders. Strictly, the only circumstances in which this is

Market value and connected persons

not so is if the shareholders are genuinely in dispute and no one shareholder or block of shareholders alone has control.

II Computation

Chapter 5

Consideration

General

The CGT legislation does not in general terms state how the consideration received on a disposal is to be determined. In certain cases, it deems the consideration to be a particular figure, usually either market value or such amount as would secure that neither a loss nor gain accrues to the disponor. But otherwise, what constitutes the consideration, and its amount, fall to be determined by common sense. About the only rule which is laid down is that if the consideration cannot be valued at all, market value is substituted (CGTA 1979 s.29A(1)(b); see p 17).

Amount of consideration

If the consideration is money, the money is the amount of the consideration. If it is anything other than money, then it has to be valued. This point emerges from cases on contingent liabilities where the value of a contingent right had to be added to the immediate cash price (*Marren v Ingles* [1980] STC 500; *Marson v Marriage* [1980] STC 177). Where an asset is disposed of subject to a mortgage or charge, the liability thereby assumed by the purchaser forms part of the consideration for the disposal (CGTA 1979 s.23(3)).

For CGT purposes, the gross amount of the consideration is brought into the computation. Costs incurred in making the disposal are relieved as allowable expenditure (see p 29).

If a vendor is indemnified by the purchaser against any tax due on the disposal, or if the purchaser specifically undertakes to pay the tax, such an obligation forms part of the consideration for the disposal. Strictly, this means that the actual sum paid has to be grossed up, so that the consideration for the disposal is such sum as after payment of the tax thereon will leave a net sum equal to the actual sum paid. As will be apparent this

Consideration

means the CGT is considerably greater than if the tax is simply born by the vendor. Such a result is avoided if it can be argued either that the bargain is not at arm's length or that the indemnity is consideration which cannot be valued. In these circumstances market value falls to be substituted (CGTA 1979 s.29A; see p 17).

Value shifting (CGTA 1979, s.26)

In certain situations the Revenue are allowed to increase the consideration for CGT purposes by such amount as appears just and reasonable. They are entitled to do this if the following conditions are satisfied:

(1) the value of the asset disposed of has been materially reduced;
(2) a tax-free benefit has been conferred on the taxpayer or someone connected with him;
(3) the reduction in value and the tax-free benefit are the result of a scheme or arrangement.

When the scheme or arrangement involves a reduction in the value of shares in one company owned by another company, the Revenue cannot adjust the consideration for the shares unless certain further conditions are met. These rules are described on p 68 below.

Income receipts (CGTA 1979 s.31)

The following are excluded from the consideration in any CGT computation:

(1) any money or money's worth charged to income tax as the income of the taxpayer;
(2) any receipts taken into account in computing income, gains, profits or losses for income tax purposes.

These exclusions are themselves subject to two exceptions in that they do not exclude either:

(1) a balancing charge or the disposal value of machinery or plant, under the capital allowances legislation; or
(2) the capitalised value of –
   (a) rentcharges;
   (b) ground annuals or feu duties;
   (c) rights of any other nature to income payments or payments in the nature of income over a period.

Contingent consideration (CGTA 1979 ss.40 and 41)

These rules are the means by which CGT is restricted to capital gains. A revenue asset, such as a trading stock, can in theory give rise to a chargeable gain if for some reason the proceeds of its sale are not fully brought into an income computation. But in practice most cases of this kind are relieved by the various chattel exemptions, described in chapter 15.

Although rent is a right to income over a period, the capitalised value of rent does not count as consideration for CGT purposes. The grant of a lease is a part disposal and, under special rules relating to leases, the right to rent is part of the retained asset (CGTA 1979 Sch 3 para 2)

Deferred consideration (CGTA 1979 s.40)

Consideration has to be brought into account in full, without any discount for any postponement of the right to receive it and without regard to the risk of it being irrecoverable. If in fact it turns out to be irrecoverable, any tax assessed is discharged or repaid.

Tax on deferred consideration may be paid by instalments if three conditions are satisfied:

(1) the consideration is payable by instalments;
(2) the instalments are spread over at least 18 months; and
(3) the taxpayer would suffer undue hardship if he had to pay all the tax at the normal time.

Contingent consideration (CGTA 1979 ss.40 and 41)

Contingent consideration is consideration payable after the disposal but only if some condition is satisfied. If the consideration is fixed in amount it is treated in the same way as deferred consideration, and so is brought into account in full without regard to the contingency. Should it subsequently become clear that the condition on which it is payable will not be satisfied, an appropriate discharge or repayment of tax is made.

If the amount of the contingent consideration is not fixed, then the contingency extends both to amount and liability. In these circumstances the contingency is valued, and only the value of the contingent right forms part of the consideration (*Marson v Marriage* [1980] STC 177).

But this right is thereafter itself an asset. If and at such time as the condition for the contingent payment is satisfied, the extra

Consideration

money is a capital sum derived from an asset, namely the contingent right (*Marren v Ingles* [1980] STC 500; see p 12). The payment thus counts as a disposal and a gain normally accrues. A loss can be claimed if the condition is not satisfied for then the contingent right has become valueless, thereby enabling the taxpayer to elect for a deemed disposal (CGTA 1979 s.22; see p 14).

The law on contingent consideration is important in practice, for there are many commercial situations in which part of the consideration for a disposal is contingent. One example arises on the sale of land, where the vendor may seek an additional payment if the purchaser secures a valuable planning permission. Another instance occurs on the sale of a company, where the parties may wish part of the purchase price to be contingent on the company attaining a certain level of profitability over a given period of years.

The present law on contingent consideration is unsatisfactory in at least three respects:

(1) If the contingent consideration is fixed in amount the taxpayer must pay tax on consideration he has not yet received and may never receive. Although if he never receives it, a discharge may be claimed, the taxpayer still has to make a loan to the Revenue.

(2) If the amount of the contingent consideration is not fixed, the taxpayer must pay tax on more than the cash amount he receives, for the contingency has to be valued. He will only recover this tax if the condition is not satisfied where (i) he claims a loss, and (ii) he has gains in the same or a later year of assessment against which the loss may be relieved.

(3) Because a contingent right to uncertain consideration is a separate asset, reliefs applicable to the original asset are not available if and when the condition is satisfied. This is particularly significant where the original asset is a private residence qualifying for the private residence exemption, a business asset attracting roll-over relief, or shares disposed of in a share for share exchange (for shares see further p 127).

Leases (CGTA 1979 Sch 3)

As noted above, the grant of a lease is part disposal, and the right to rent forms part of the retained asset. Any premium paid counts as consideration for the part disposal, but if no premium is taken, no consideration is received for CGT purposes and the lease is accordingly without CGT consequences. If part of the premium is taxed as income under TA 1988 s.34, that part counts as rent, and so forms part of the retained asset in the part disposal computation.

Certain sums paid by the tenant during the currency of a lease are deemed to be premiums:

(a) sums paid in lieu of rent;
(b) sums paid to secure a surrender of the lease;
(c) sums paid in consideration of a waiver or variation of the terms of the lease.

Options (CGTA 1979 s.137)

The tax treatment of option monies depends on whether the option is exercised. If it is, the grant of the option and the exercise are treated as a single transaction, taking place on the date of exercise. The option monies, therefore, form part of the consideration for the substantive disposal.

Should the option not be exercised, the option monies are treated as consideration given for a newly created asset, namely the option itself. This new asset has no base value and, accordingly, the gain is chargeable in its entirety with no indexation allowance. The same rule applies to a deposit taken on a bilateral contract if the contract is not completed.

Chapter 6

Allowable Expenditure

Introduction (CGTA 1979 s.32)

The deductions which are allowed in computing an unindexed gain fall under three heads:

(1) acquisition cost;
(2) enhancement expenditure;
(3) the incidental costs of the disposal.

Acquisition cost (CGTA 1979 s.32 (1)(a))

Three forms of acquisition cost are allowed:

(1) the amount or value of the consideration given by the taxpayer wholly and exclusively for the acquisition of the asset;
(2) the incidental costs of the acquisition;
(3) if the taxpayer did not acquire the asset, any expenditure wholly and exclusively incurred by him in providing it.

The phrase 'wholly and exclusively' does not entirely mean what it says, for apportionments can be made and expenditure with a dual purpose has been allowed (CGTA 1979 s.43; *IRC v Richards Executors* [1971] 1 All ER 785). But for such expenditure to be allowable, the non-allowable purpose must be subsidiary or ancillary (*Cleveleys Investment Trust v IRC* [1975] STC 457).

Where the value of one asset is derived from another asset in the same ownership, the allowable expenditure on the first asset can include an appropriate proportion of the expenditure on the second asset (CGTA 1979 s.36). But for this provision to apply, the assets must have been merged or divided, their nature must have changed, or rights or interest over assets must have been created or extinguished. This provision has been described as obscure and it has been restrictively construed (*Aberdeen Construction Group Ltd v IRC* [1978] STC 127; *Bayley v Rogers* [1980] STC 544).

Enhancement expenditure (CGTA 1979 s.32(1)(b))

Two forms of enhancement expenditure are allowed:
(1) expenditure on improvements which satisfies the following four conditions:-
   (a) it was wholly and exclusively incurred on the asset;
   (b) it was incurred by or on behalf of the taxpayer;
   (c) it was incurred for the purpose of enhancing the value of the asset;
   (d) it is reflected in the state or nature of the asset at the time of the disposal;
(2) expenditure wholly and exclusively incurred in establishing, preserving or defending title to the asset.

As will be apparent, expenditure on improvements requires a subjective test to be satisfied when the expenditure is incurred and an objective one when the asset is disposed of. The latter requires the expenditure to be reflected in the state or nature of the asset and thus excludes two important kinds of expenditure. The first is expenditure which was once, but is no longer, reflected in the state or nature of the asset, and the second is expenditure which is solely reflected in the value of the asset. In practice the Revenue appear not to apply this exclusion strictly and they have conceded that a payment made to a statutory tenant to obtain vacant possession counts as expenditure on improvements (*Chaney v Watkis* [1986] STC 89).

The second head of enhancement expenditure, preservation, etc, of title, has generated a surprising amount of case law. It has been held to include the cost to executors of making the inventory and valuations necessary for a grant of probate (*IRC v Richards Executors* [1971] 1 All ER 785). But it does not extend to a premium paid on the variation of a trust or sums paid by a residuary beneficiary to discharge the estate's liabilities (*Allison v Murray* [1975] STC 534; *Passant v Jackson* [1986] STC 164).

Incidental costs (CGTA 1979 s.32(2))

Incidental costs comprise the following:

Allowable expenditure

(1) professional charges;
(2) the costs of any conveyance or transfer, including stamp duty;
(3) advertising costs;
(4) the costs of any valuations and apportionments required for CGT purposes.

Income expenditure (CGTA 1979 s.33)

Even if expenditure falls within the categories described above, it is disallowed if it is income expenditure. The rules are somewhat convoluted, but in broad terms all normal income costs such as repairs, rent, and maintenance cannot be deducted. Improvements are not excluded and nor are works required to put a new asset into a usable state, for these are treated as capital in computing trading profits (*Law Shipping Co Ltd v IRC* (1923) 12 TC 621).

Capital allowances and renewals allowances (CGTA 1979 s.34)

When it comes to computing a gain, expenditure which has qualified for a capital or renewals allowance is fully allowable. But this rule does not apply if and insofar as a loss is created since otherwise the same loss would be relieved against both Income Tax and CGT.

The capital allowances taken into account for these purposes include any balancing allowance made on the disposal. If the disposal or any previous event occasions a balancing charge, the charge is deducted from the capital allowances taken into account in computing a loss.

Example

Cost of asset	£10,000
Capital allowances	£ 4,000
Written down value	£ 6,000
Consideration	£ 9,000
Balancing charge	£ 3,000

The capital gains position is:

Consideration		£ 9,000
Cost of acquisition	£10,000	
Less: capital allowances	£ 4,000	
	£ 6,000	

Part disposals (CGTA 1979 s.35)

Plus balancing charge	£ 3,000	£ 9,000
Unindexed gain		NIL

Part disposals (CGTA 1979 s.35)

Where part only of an asset is disposed of, the allowable expenditure attributable to the whole asset must be apportioned between the part disposed of and the part remaining. This apportionment is effected by the fraction $\frac{A}{A+B}$ where A is the amount or value of the consideration for the disposal and B is the market value of the property undisposed of.

Example
The cost of an asset in May 1983 was £10,000. Part of the asset was sold in June 1989 for £12,000, when the value of the remainder was £8,000. Incidental costs of disposal were £500.

Consideration for part disposal		£12,000
Less: cost of part disposed of:		
$\frac{£12,000}{£12,000+£8,000} \times £10,000 = £6,000$		
Cost of disposal	£500	£ 6,500
Unindexed gain		£ 5,500

Cost of part of asset retained £10,000 – £6,000 = £4,000

In some cases expenditure will have been incurred which is solely referable to the part of the asset disposed of or alternatively solely referable to the part retained. If this is the position the apportionment just described does not apply and the expenditure is deductible only from the part to which it was attributable.

Some part disposals are not treated as disposals at all, and instead, the consideration for the disposal is deducted from the acquisition cost of the retained asset. This treatment is inter alia accorded to the following kinds of part disposal:

(a) small capital distributions from a company (CGTA 1979 s.72(2); see p 65);
(b) part disposals of land, if the consideration is less than £20,000 and the part disposed of represents less than one fifth of the total value of the holding (CGTA 1979 s.107);
(c) insurance monies applied in reinstatement (CGTA 1979 s.21; see p 122).

Allowable expenditure

Wasting assets (CGTA 1979 ss.37-39)

Wasting assets are assets with a predictable life of 50 years or less (see p 8) Wasting assets which do not qualify for capital allowances are subject to special rules requiring the allowable expenditure to be written off over the life of the asset. These rules vary, depending upon whether the asset is a lease of land or not.

If a wasting asset is not a lease of land, allowable expenditure is written off at a uniform rate on a straight-line basis. The mechanics are that a deduction is made both from the acquisition cost and the enhancement expenditure.

The deduction from the aquisition cost is arrived at by first subtracting the residual or scrap value of the asset from its acquisition cost. The fraction $\frac{T(1)}{L}$ is then applied to this amount and the resultant figure is the deduction. In the fraction L is the predictable life of the asset at the time of its acquisition, and T(1) is the period of the taxpayer's ownership.

The deduction in any item of enhancement expenditure is ascertained by multiplying the amount of that item by the fraction $\frac{T(2)}{L-(T(1)-T(2))}$. In this fraction L and T(1) have the meaning given above, and T(2) is the period between the date of the enhancement expenditure and the date of the disposal. Should the expenditure increase the residual value of the asset, the residual value so increased is the value taken into account in ascertaining the deduction from the acquisition cost.

Example

A wasting asset was purchased on 1 May 1982 for £15,000. At that date the asset had a predictable life of fifteen years (L) and an estimated scrap value of £1,000. On 1 May 1985, £5,000 was incurred on improving the asset, which was reflected in the state of the asset but did not alter the estimated scrap value. On 1 May 1989 the asset is sold for £22,000. Incidental costs of diposal were £650.

The chargeable gain is:

Consideration: £22,000

Cost: £20,000

Less: $(£15,000-£1,000) \times \frac{6\text{yrs (T1)}}{15\text{yrs(L)}}$ = £5,600

$£5000 \times \frac{3\text{yrs (T2)}}{15\text{yrs (L)} - (6\text{yrs(T1)} - 3\text{yrs(T2)})}$ = £1,250 £6,850

£13,150

Leases (CGTA 1979 Sch 3 para 1)

Incidental costs of disposal	£650	£13,800
Unindexed gain		£8,200

Leases (CGTA 1979 Sch 3 para 1)

A lease of land is a wasting asset if the unexpired term is less than 50 years (see p 9). Expenditure is not written off at a uniform rate, but instead the allowable expenditure is reduced by specified fractions.

The reduction in the acquisition cost is arrived at by multiplying the cost by $\frac{P(1) - P(3)}{P(1)}$ and the reduction in each item of expenditure on improvements is arrived at by multiplying the cost of the item by $\frac{P(2) - P(3)}{P(2)}$. In these fractions $P(1)$ is the percentage appropriate to the lease when it is acquired, $P(2)$ the appropriate percentage when the expenditure was first reflected in the nature of the lease, and $P(3)$ the appropriate percentage when the lease is disposed of. The percentages are derived from a table set out in the legislation, which gives the appropriate percentage for each full year of the unexpired term. When plotted, these percentages describe a curve, flat at the beginning, steep at the end.

The writing off of expenditure on leases is meant to reflect the realities of lease valuation, and so it does when the initial consideration for the lease is a low rent and a premium. But substantial premiums can now be paid when rack-rent leases change hands, either as key money or because the assignment takes place between reviews. The assignee who pays such a premium may himself receive a similar premium when he assigns, and this is so even if the original lease has ended and a new one has been granted under the Landlord and Tenant Act 1954. In these circumstances the writing-off of the original premium does not reflect the realities of lease valuation and deprives the assignee of expenditure which ought to be allowable.

Example

On 1 April 1982 G L Ltd acquires a 25-year lease of a shop for £25,000. It extends the shop at a cost of £10,000 which is first reflected in the nature of the lease on 1 April 1987.

On 1 April 1992 it assigns the lease for £40,000. The allowable expenditure is reduced as follows:

P(1)   Duration of lease at
       acquisition   25 years   =   £81.100

Allowable expenditure

P(3)	Duration of lease at disposal	15 years =	£61.617	
P(1) - P(3)			£19.483	
P(2)	Duration of lease from 1 April 1987	20 years	£72.770	
P(3)	Duration of lease at disposal	15 years	£61.617	
P(2) - P(3) =			£11,153	

Consideration for assignment		£40,000
Less: cost of aquisition	£25,000	
proportion not allowable $\frac{19.483}{81.100} \times £25,000$	£ 6,006	£18,994
enhancement	£10,000	
proportion not allowable $\frac{11.153}{72,770} \times £10,000$	£ 1,533	£ 8,467
Unindexed gain		£12,539

Wasting assets qualifying for capital allowances (CGTA 1979 s.39)

The rules set out above do not apply to wasting assets which have qualified for capital allowances. Gains and losses on these wasting assets are computed in the same way as for non-wasting assets which qualify for capital allowances (see p 30). Apportionments are made where assets are used only partly for the purpose of a trade, profession or vocation, or where they have been used for only part of the period from the disponor's acquisition to the date of disposal.

Chapter 7

Pooling and Identification

Introduction

Unnumbered shares and securities of the same class are indistinguishable. This does not pose computational difficulties where a holding results from a single acquisition and is comprised in a single disposal. But where this is not so, rules are needed to determine the acquisition cost of any given disposal out of the holding.

Over the years, the CGT legislation has adopted two solutions to this problem. One is pooling, which treats the holding as a single asset and so uses average cost as the acquisition cost. The other is artificial rules of identification, which identify the shares disposed of with the shares acquired on some arbitrary basis such as last-in first-out.

In the CGT legislation these rules are expressed in terms of shares and securities, for those are the principal assets to which the rules apply. But the rules also apply to all other assets of a nature to be dealt in without identifying the particular asset disposed of or acquired.

Pooling and the arbitrary rules of identification have only ever applied within single classes of shares or securities. There has never been a time when all the taxpayer's shares or all his securities have been in a single pool, or when disposals have been identified otherwise than with acquisitions of shares or securities in the same class. Shares and securities count as being in the same class if they are so treated on the Stock Exchange or would be so treated if they were quoted. If they are of the same class they are deemed to be incapable of individual identification even if in fact they are separately numbered.

Pooling and identification

History (CGTA 1979 s.65; FA 1982 s.88; FA 1985 Sch 19)

When CGT was first enacted pooling was the general rule. It applied to the following assets:

(1) all shares and corporate securities acquired after 5 April 1965;
(2) quoted shares and securities held on 6 April 1965 if the taxpayer had elected they should be pooled;
(3) other assets not able to be individually identified and acquired after 6 April 1965.

Pooling did not apply, inter alia, to the following assets:

(1) non-corporate securities such as gilts;
(2) quoted shares and securities held on 6 April which were not subject to a pooling election;
(3) unquoted shares and other unidentifiable assets held on 6 April 1965.

In 1982, the introduction of indexation occasioned the abolition of pooling. Pooling had to be abolished, because at that time, indexation did not apply to assets held for less than one year (see p 49). It was replaced by rules of identification, which applied to all shares and securities acquired on or after what is termed the 1982 date, namely 1 April 1982 for companies and 6 April 1982 for other taxpayers. These rules applied also gilts and other non-corporate securities.

The 1982 identification rules did not apply to existing pools held on the 1982 date. Instead these remained in being as single assets, but they were incapable of being added to but could only be diminished. Complicated rules applied if the pool had increased between what may be called the 1981 date and the 1982 date. The 1981 date was 1 April 1981 for companies and 6 April 1981 for individuals. The effect of the rules was that the pool was the pool as at the 1981 date, reduced by any disposals prior to the acquisitions which had increased the pool beyond its size at the 1981 date. Pools of this kind were known as reduced holdings, and shares and securities acquired in 1981-2 and not included within it were subject to special rules of identification.

In 1985, the simplification of indexation meant that pooling could be reintroduced. However, virtually all securities, known as 'Relevant Securities', were excluded from pooling, and for other assets two separate pools were created, known respectively as 1982 Holdings and New Holdings. The 1985 system was introduced with effect from what is known as the 1985 date, namely 1 April 1985 for companies and 6 April 1985 for other

New holdings (FA 1985 s.68(9) and Sch 19 paras 8–10)

taxpayers. The system is the system which remains in force today, although some of the rules which apply to 1982 holdings are not material if the taxpayer has elected for 1982 rebasing to apply to all his assets (see p 41).

New Holdings (FA 1985 s.68(9) and Sch 19 paras 8–10)

The following assets are pooled as 'new holdings':
 (1) quoted and unquoted shares;
 (2) securities which are not 'relevant securities';
 (3) other assets not able to be individually identified, except for material interests in 'offshore funds', which count as 'relevant securities'.

In relation to any given class of these assets the 'new holding' consists of all such assets acquired on or after the 1982 date. The 'new holding' is treated as a single asset, growing when new assets are acquired and diminishing when they are sold. The acquisition cost of this composite asset is the aggregate of the acquisition costs of each acquisition, and the disposal of some assets out of the holding is treated as a part disposal. On such a part disposal, the acquisition cost of the part disposed of is determined by the normal part disposal rules, and the balance is carried forward to the rest of the holding.

New holdings came into being in one of two ways. Either the first acquisition was after the 1985 date, or assets of the relevant class were already held by the taxpayer on that date. In the latter event, the initial new holding was such of the assets as had been acquired since the 1982 date, and not indentified with disposals before the 1985 date under the 1982 rules of identification.

In certain circumstances assets do not join a new holding. This principally happens if an acquisition is on the same day as a disposal or if it is followed by a disposal within ten days (FA 1985 Sch 19 para 18; CGTA 1979 s.66). But shares and securities are also excluded from a new holding if the taxpayer is a company holding 2 per cent or more of all the shares or securities in the class concerned, and the acquisition takes place within the prescribed period of a disposal (F(No 2) A 1975 s.58). The prescribed period is one month either side of the disposal, or, if the disposal is not through a stock exchange, six months.

Shares are pooled separately if they are issued to an employee on terms restricting his right to dispose of them. A separate pool also exists if shares are acquired in a personal equity plan (see p 90).

Pooling and identification

1982 Holdings (FA 1982 Sch 13 paras 8-9; FA 1985 Sch 19 paras 6-7)

1982 holdings are the pools built up under the original pooling rules, which were preserved when pooling was abolished in 1982. Since the 1982 date, these holdings have only been able to be diminished. Any acquisition of assets of the same class now constitutes or is added to a new holding.

As with new holdings, the part disposal rules apply on any disposal out of a 1982 holding. Provided 1982 rebasing applies, the acquisition cost of the holding is the market value of the holding on 31 March 1982 (FA 1988 s.96; see chapter 8). If under the 1982 rules, the single asset was a reduced holding, the 1982 holding includes both the reduced holding and any assets acquired between the 1981 and the 1982 dates which were not identified with disposals before the 1985 date.

As noted above, the original pooling rules excluded government securities but applied to all company securities. Most of the latter fall within the term relevant security, but they are not excluded from being pooled in a 1982 holding. Accordingly such securities acquired before the 1982 date are pooled, but those acquired thereafter are not.

Because of the original pooling rules, 1982 holdings exclude unquoted shares held on 6 April 1965. They also exclude quoted shares and securities held on that date unless election has been made to the contrary. Such elections originally had to be made in respect either of all the taxpayer's ordinary shares or of all his fixed interest securities and preference shares. The election had to be made within two years of the first disposal of securities of the kind to which it related after 19 March 1968. By the 1985 date, the original time for most such elections had long since past. But the 1985 Finance Act conferred a new right to make such elections, as respects whatever quoted shares and securities the taxpayer still retained from 1965 (FA 1985 Sch 19 para 6).

If a taxpayer has both a new holding and a 1982 holding, disposals are identified with the new holding first. If he has held some of the assets since 1965, and they are not quoted shares and securities included in a 1982 holding, disposals are not identified with those assets until both the new holding and the 1982 holding have been exhausted.

Relevant Securities (FA 1982 s.88)

The term 'Relevant Securities' means the following:

Relevant Securities (FA 1982 s.88)

(1) securities, as defined for the purposes of the accrued income scheme (TA 1988 s.710);
(2) deep discount securities within the meaning of TA 1988 Sch 4;
(3) material interests in non-qualifying offshore funds (TA 1988 ss.757–764).

This definition means that Relevant Securities embrace virtually all securities, for the accrued income scheme definition is extemely wide. It is in substantially the same terms as the definition of security in CGTA 1979 s.82 and includes loan stock and similar securities, whether British or foreign, and whether issued by a company or by a public sector body.

Relevant Securities acquired after the 1982 date are not pooled, but remain subject to the 1982 rules of identification. Under these rules, securities disposed of are identified first with acquisitions within the previous twelve months on a first-in first-out basis, and then with earlier acquisitions on a last-in first-out basis.

Most Relevant Securities are either gilts or qualifying corporate bonds. As such they are exempt, which means that the identification rules relating to Relevant Securities are now of restricted practical application (see p 86).

Chapter 8

1982 Rebasing

General (FA 1988 s.96)

1982 rebasing applies to assets which the taxpayer has owned since 31 March 1982. Such assets are deemed to have been reacquired by the taxpayer on 31 March 1982 at their then market value, and accordingly, in computing any gain or loss, the 1982 value is substituted for the actual pre 1982 expenditure. 1982 rebasing was introduced in 1988, and so has applied in computing gains and losses accruing on disposals on or after 6 April 1988.

The effect of 1982 rebasing is to exempt gains accruing before 31 March 1982. Prior to 6 April 1988 the base date for CGT was 6 April 1965, the date when the tax was first introduced. Gains accruing before then were relieved either by a deemed reacquisition on 6 April 1965 or by straight-line apportionment (CGTA 1979 Sch 5). It is to be noted that the latter, which tended to favour taxpayers, has not been incorporated into 1982 rebasing: the new rebasing is achieved solely by deemed reacquisition.

A special rule applies where the taxpayer made a part disposal between 31 March 1982 and 5 April 1988 and disposes of the retained asset thereafter. Here the gain on the disposal of the retained asset is computed by reference to the amount of the 1982 value which would have been carried forward had rebasing applied on the part disposal.

Special rules also apply in practice to shares (SP 5/89; ESC dated 25 May 1989). In determining the 1982 value of any shares a taxpayer is allowed to treat unpooled shares acquired before 1965 as part of the same holding as shares of the same class acquired between 1965 and 1982. He is also allowed to include in his holding any shares of the same class as he has acquired since 31 March 1982 on a no gain/no loss disposal. The meaning of no gain/no loss disposals is explained below (p 44), and the effect of these rules is to allow the 1982 value of shares to be computed on a control basis in certain cases where this would not otherwise be so.

Rebasing excluded (FA 1988 s.96(3) and Sch 8 para 10)

The election (FA 1988 s.96(5) and Sch 8 paras 1 and 13)

A taxpayer may elect for 1982 rebasing to apply to all his assets owned since before 31 March 1982. If he does so elect, rebasing applies in computing gains and losses on all those assets. The only exceptions are plant and machinery qualifying for capital allowances, assets used in a mineral working trade and oil licences.

A taxpayer may make a rebasing election at any time before 5 April 1990. If he fails to do so then he has a further bite of the cherry in that he can also make the election within two years of the year of assessment or accounting period in which he first makes a relevant disposal. A relevant disposal is any disposal to which rebasing applies, and thus any disposal of an asset owned since before 31 March 1982. In practice certain disposals of exempt assets do not count as relevant disposals (SP 2/89) and the two-year period, but not the 1990 limit, can be extended by the Revenue.

Subsidiary companies in a group normally cannot make an election and in general they are bound by any election made by the parent. These rules are discussed below on p 67.

Rebasing excluded (FA 1988 s.96(3) and Sch 8 para 10)

Where the taxpayer has not made a rebasing election, rebasing does not apply on every disposal of assets owned since 31 March 1982. It is excluded if:

(a) an indexed gain accrues with rebasing and either a smaller gain or a loss accrues without; or
(b) an indexed loss accrues with rebasing and either a smaller loss or a gain accrues without.

Where the gain or loss without rebasing is smaller than that with rebasing, the former is taken as the gain or loss for CGT purposes and rebasing is thus totally excluded. If there is gain without rebasing, and a loss without, or vice versa, neither the 1982 value nor the pre 1982 expenditure apply and instead the asset is treated as acquired at such figure as produces neither loss nor gain.

In comparing gains and losses, the comparison is, as noted, between indexed gains and losses (FA 1982 s.86). The indexation allowance is not affected by the applicability or otherwise of rebasing. It is based on the 1982 value of the asset unless substitution of actual pre 1982 expenditure would produce a greater allowance (see p 51).

1982 rebasing

Example 1 - gain with rebasing
Mr Smith acquires three assets before 1982. Asset A costs £50, Asset B £110, and Asset C £150. Each asset is worth £100 in 1982 and is sold in 1989 for £200. The indexation factor from 1982 is assumed to be 0.4.

(i) Gain on each asset with rebasing

Unindexed gain 200-100	100
Indexation (.4 × 100)	(40)
Indexed gain	60

(ii) Rebasing excluded

    (a)   Asset A (pre 1982 expenditure 50)

Unindexed gain 200-50	150
Indexation (.4 × 100)	(40)
Gain	110

Rebasing applies
Gain 60

    (b)   Asset B (pre 1982 expenditure 110)

Unindexed gain 200-110	90
Indexation (.4 × 110)	(44)
Indexed gain	46

Rebasing excluded
Gain 44

    (c)   Asset C (pre 1982 expenditure 150)

Unindexed gain 200-150	50
Indexation (.4 × 150)	(60)
Indexed loss	(10)

Rebasing excluded
No gain/no loss acquisition

Example 2 - loss with rebasing
Mr Jones acquires Assets D, E and F before 1982. Asset D costs £200, Asset E £75 and Asset F £5. Each asset is worth £100 in 1982 and is sold in 1989 for £50. The indexation factor is 0.4.

(i) Loss on each asset with rebasing

Unindexed loss 50-100	(50)
Indexation (.4 × 100)	(40)
Indexed loss	(90)

(ii) Rebasing excluded

    (a)   Asset D (pre 1982 expenditure 200)

Unindexed loss 50-200	(150)

Should taxpayers make the election?

       Indexation (200 × .4)   (80)
       Indexed loss   (230)
Rebasing applies
Loss (90)

(b)   Asset E (pre 1982 expenditure 75)
        Unindexed loss 50-75   (25)
        Indexation (100 × .4)   (40)
        Indexed loss   (65)
Rebasing excluded
Loss (65)

(c)   Asset F (pre 1982 expenditure 5)
        Unindexed gain 50-5   45
        Indexation (100 × .4)   (40)
        Indexed gain   5
Rebasing excluded
No gain/no loss acquisition

Where the asset was acquired before 6 April 1965 and straight-line apportionment applies in the absence of rebasing, the gain or loss without rebasing is the gain or loss after time apportionment. If on the 1965 base date deemed reacquisition applies, and under the rules relating to that reacquisition it is treated as a no gain/no loss acquisition, it is also so treated for 1982 rebasing purposes.

Should taxpayers make the election?

There is one obvious argument in favour of making an election, namely that it removes the necessity of computing the indexed gain or loss without rebasing. This argument has led many commentators to presume in favour of an election, but matters are not as simple as that and each taxpayer should consider whether an election will in fact be advantageous for him.

There are certain situations where an election is clearly wrong. One such arises if (i) several taxpayers purchased all the share capital of a company before 1982; (ii) each took only a minority holding; and (iii) the overall value of the company showed little increase prior to 1982. Here, the acquisition cost will be based on an assets value, whereas the 1982 value of each taxpayer's holding will be arrived at on a minority basis. Plainly, in these circumstances rebasing will be most unattractive.

Another special situation covers assets acquired before 1965 to which time apportionment applies. Since time apportionment applies on a straight-line basis its effect is to exempt gains which have in reality accrued pre 1965. Time apportionment is an argument against electing for 1982 rebasing in so far as any asset was (i) acquired well before 1965, (ii) showed relatively little increase until 1982, and (iii) has grown significantly in value since then.

Whatever the eventual decision is, it should be taken before 6 April 1990. There are two reasons for this. First, the breadth of the term disposal means the first relevant disposal may be missed so that the alternative two-year limit expires without action having been taken. Second, in deciding whether to elect, 1982 values are all important, and these will be easier to obtain and more convincing if action is taken sooner rather than later.

No gain/no loss disposals (FA 1988 s.96(3)(d) and Sch 8 para 1)

No gain/no loss disposals are disposals where neither a gain nor a loss accrues to the disponor and instead the recipient is treated as acquiring the asset at the recipient's base cost. The prime examples are disposals between spouses, disposals between group members and disposals on a reconstruction or amalgamation (see pp 61, 66, and 127). No gain/no loss disposals are now listed for the purposes of rebasing and indexation (FA 1985 s.68; FA 1988 Sch 8 para 1).

In the absence of special provision an asset acquired before 31 March 1982 and subject to a no gain/no loss disposal between then and 5 April 1988 would lose the benefit of rebasing, for the recipient would not have owned it on 31 March 1982. In reality this situation is covered by the legislation, for the recipient is treated as having owned the asset on 31 March 1982. Accordingly, no gain/no loss disposals between 1982 and 1988 do not cause rebasing to be lost.

Where the no gain/no loss disposal take place on or after 6 April 1988, the recipient is also treated as having held the asset on 31 March 1982 if the disponor did. If the disponor has made a rebasing election, that election applies to the no gain/no loss disposal, and so a deemed 1982 reacquisition necessarily applies to the recipient regardless of whether he has made an election. But if the disponor does not make an election, rebasing is ipso facto excluded on all his no gain/no loss disposals (FA 1988 s.96(3)(d)). In these circumstances, 1982 rebasing can be displaced on the recipient's subsequent disposal in the same circumstances as on any other disposal he makes. In other words it is displaced

Held-over and rolled-over gains (FA 1988 Sch 9)

if (i) he has not made an election, and (ii) rebasing would increase the indexed gain or loss or turns one into the other.

Special rules apply to elections and two categories of no gain/no loss disposal, namely those between spouses and group members. Where a no gain/no loss disposal in one of these categories takes place on or after 6 April 1988, the asset concerned is governed by the election or non-election of the disponor rather than that of the recipient. This rule prevents spouses and groups from arranging their assets so that assets benefitting from an election are held by the spouse or group member who has elected, and assets not so benefitting are held by a spouse or group member that has not. It might be thought that the single election rule for groups means this rule has little application to them; but this is not so, for a group can include members not covered by the election or non-election of the parent (see p 67).

Held-over and rolled-over gains (FA 1988 Sch 9)

An anomaly arises in the interaction of 1982 rebasing with hold-over relief and roll-over relief. These reliefs are enumerated in chapters 18–20. The main example of hold-over relief is the relief for gifts and the main example of roll-over relief is the relief for the replacement of business assets.

In the case of hold-over relief the anomaly arises if (i) the disponor owned the asset on 31 March 1982, (ii) the hold-over disposal occurred between then and 5 April 1988, and (iii) the recipient disposes of the asset after 6 April 1988. In the case of roll-over relief the anomaly arises where (i) the old asset was acquired before 31 March 1982, (ii) the roll-over disposal occurs between then and 5 April 1988, and (iii) the new asset is disposed of after 6 April 1988. In all these cases the anomaly is simply that part of the gain on the post-6 April 1988 disposal accrued before 31 March 1982 and yet rebasing does not apply because the taxpayer making that disposal did not then own the asset.

The obvious solution to this problem would have been to deem the gifted or the new asset to have been owned by the post-1988 disponor on 31 March 1982. But this course has not been adopted and instead a quite arbitrary relief applies. The amount otherwise deducted from the acquisition cost of the donee or (as the case may be) of the new asset is reduced by half.

The conditions which have to be satisfied for this relief to apply are as follows:

1982 rebasing

(1) the roll-over or hold-over disposal occurs between 31 March 1982 and 5 April 1988;
(2) the old asset or (as the case may be) the gifted asset was acquired before 31 March 1982;
(3) the new asset or (as the case may be) the gifted asset is disposed of after 6 April 1988.

This relief only applies if it is claimed. The claim must be made within two years of the year of assessment or accounting period is which the post-1988 disposal is made.

Where the disposal between 1982–88 was a roll-over relief disposal, it is not necessary for the new asset to have been acquired before 6 April 1988. This is significant where the relief concerned is that applying on the replacement of business assets or the compulsory acquisition of land, for here up to three years can elapse before the new asset need be acquired (see pp 116 and 121). Accordingly, taxpayers who disposed of assets potentially attracting one or other of these reliefs before 6 April 1988 can effectively exempt half the gain by acquiring new assets, providing the acquisition takes place within three years of the disposal of the old.

Example 3 (hold-over relief)
Mr X acquires an asset in 1972 for £100. In 1982 it is worth £200. In 1986 it is worth £300 and he gives it to his son, Mr Y, and they elect for hold-over relief to apply. In 1989 Mr Y sells the asset for £500.

Indexation factors (assume):
1982–6   0.1
1986–9   0.3

If no claim made under Schedule 9

1986 gift	1986 market value		300
	Allowable expenditure		(100)
	Indexation (.1 x 200)		(20)
	Indexed held-over gain		180
1989 sale	Proceeds		500
	Allowable expenditure	300	
	held-over gain	(180)	(120)
	Indexation (.3 x 120)		(36)
	Indexed gain		344

If a claim is made under Schedule 9

1985 gift   as above

Postponed gains (FA 1988 Sch 9)

1989 sale	Proceeds		500
	Allowable expenditure	300	
	1/2 held-over gain	(90)	(210)
	Indexation (.3 x 210)		(63)
	Indexed gain		227

Example 4 (roll-over relief)
X Limited acquires the old asset in 1975 for £1,000. It is worth £2,000 in 1982. It sells the old asset in 1986 for £3,000 and buys the new asset for £3,000. It sells the new asset in 1989 for £5,000.

Indexation factors   as above

If no claim made under Schedule 9

1986 sale	Proceeds		3,000
	Allowable expenditure		(1,000)
	Indexation (.1 x 2,000)		(200)
	Rolled-over indexed gain		1,800
1989 sale	Proceeds		5,000
	Allowable expenditure	3,000	
	Rolled-over gain	(1,800)	(1,200)
	Indexation (.3 x 1,200)		(360)
	Indexed gain		3,660

If claim is made under Schedule 9

1986 sale	as above		
1989 sale	Proceeds		5000
	Allowable expenditure	3,000	
	1/2 rolled-over gain	(900)	(2,100)
	Indexation (.3 x 2100)		(630)
	Indexed gain		2,270

Postponed gains (FA 1988 Sch 9)

The arbitrary relief for held-over and rolled-over gains applies to another quite different situation, namely that where postponed gains become chargeable on the happening of some subsequent event. The main examples are the charge on held-over gains when the donee migrates, the charge when a company leaves a group and the charge when the new assets in a roll-over claim are depreciating assets.

Under the arbitrary relief, the postponed gain is reduced by half if the following conditions are satisfied:

1982 rebasing

(1) the postponed gain accrued before 6 April 1988;
(2) the asset on which it accrued was acquired before 31 March 1982;
(3) the event triggering the charged occurs after 6 April 1988;
(4) a claim is made.

Unfortunately, the original Schedule 9 treatment of postponed gains was not complete for certain postponed gains chargeable after 6 April 1988 accrued *before* 31 March 1982. In these circumstances it is now provided that the whole postponed gain drops out of charge (FA 1989 Sch 15 para 1). This is backdated to 6 April 1988.

Chapter 9

Indexation

Introduction

The basic CGT computational rules require gains and losses to be computed in purely money terms (CGTA 1979 Part II, Chapter II). Such gains and losses are known as unindexed gains and losses and, until 1982, they were the basis on which tax was charged. This was widely regarded as unjust, for the rampant inflation of the 1970s meant that in real terms CGT had become a tax on capital rather than a tax on gains.

A measure of indexation was conceded in 1982 (FA 1982 ss.86 and 87). It was unsatisfactory, for it did not apply to losses, it required assets to be held for at least a year, and it did not extend to pre-1982 inflation. The first two of these defects were remedied in 1985 (FA 1985 s.68), and the third has been cured by 1982 rebasing.

The allowance (FA 1982 s.86)

Indexation could have been achieved by expressing all items of allowable expenditure in terms of their values at the date of the disposal. In reality, this has not been done, and instead indexation is effected by the indexation allowance. This is applied to the unindexed gain or loss to give what is called the gain or loss for the purposes of CGTA 1979.

If the disposal has thrown up an unindexed gain, the allowance is deducted from the gain, and, should the allowance exceed the gain, the excess creates a loss. Should the disposal be at a loss, the indexation allowance simply increases the loss. If the disposal is one where neither a loss nor a gain is treated as accruing, the indexation allowance is added to the allowable expenditure, and the disposal becomes one which, after application of the indexation allowance, results in neither a loss nor a gain.

Indexation

Calculation of the allowance (FA 1982 s.87)

The indexation allowance is the sum of the indexed rises in each item of allowable expenditure. For these purposes, allowable expenditure means acquisition cost and enhancement expenditure, as described on pp 28-9. For obvious reasons, the incidental costs of the disposal are excluded.

To arrive at the indexed rise for an item of expenditure, it is necessary to ascertain the Retail Prices Index for two months. The first index figure, RD, is the index figure for the month in which the disposal occurs and the second figure, RI, is the index for the month in which the expenditure was incurred. For these purposes, acquisition expenditure is treated as incurred at the date when the asset is treated as aquired for CGT purposes (see p 11). Enhancement expenditure is treated as incurred when it became due and payable.

When RD and RI have been arrived at, the difference between them is expressed as a decimal of RI. The expenditure is then multiplied by this decimal, and the resultant figure is the indexed rise for that item of expenditure.

In theory calculation of indexed rises could be time-consuming, particularly as the Retail Prices Index was rebased on 1 January 1987. In practice matters are greatly simplified by the Revenue, who publish and regularly update a table showing, for each RD month, the decimal to be applied to items of expenditure incurred in all RI months since March 1982. The Revenue refer to these decimals as indexed rises, and, although this is technically incorrect, it is a convenient shorthand.

Example 1

Mr Smith purchases an investment property in January 1987 at a cost of £75,000. In September 1987, he spent a further £50,000 on the construction of an extension to the building. The building was sold for £200,000 in March 1988.

Details of the retail price index are as follows:

January 1987	100.0
September 1987	102.4
March 1988	104.1

The indexed rises are as follows:-

RI January 1987/RD March 1988
$$\frac{104.1 - 100.00}{104.1} = 0.041$$

Assets held on 31 March 1982 (FA 1985 s.68(4))

RI September 1987/RD March 1988
$$\frac{104.1 - 102.4}{102.4} = 0.017$$

Calculation of indexation allowance:

Purchase January 1987 0.041 x £75,000 =	£ 3,075
Improvement September 1987 0.017 x £50,000 =	£ 850
Indexation allowance	£ 3,925

Capital gains tax computation:

Sale proceeds	£200,000
Less: cost (£75,000 + £50,000)	£125,000
	£ 75,000
Less: indexation allowance	£3,925
Gain	£ 71,075

Example 2
The facts are the same as in Example 1, except that the sale proceeds amounted to £120,000.

Capital gains tax computation:

Sale proceeds	£120,000
Less: cost	£125,000
	£ 5,000
Less: indexation allowance	£ 3,925
Allowable loss	£ 8,925

Assets held on 31 March 1982 (FA 1985 s.68(4))

For the indexation purposes, assets acquired before 31 March 1982 are treated as aquired at market value on that date. This means that all actual expenditure incurred before that date is ignored and, instead, it is represented in the indexation allowance by the indexed rise on the 1982 value.

This rule is displaced if the aggregate indexed rises on the actual pre-1982 expenditure exceed the indexed rise on the 1982 value. In many cases they might, but for the fact that the RI month for the pre-1982 expenditure has to be March 1982 rather than the month in which the expenditure was in fact incurred. This means that the indexed rises for such expenditure are computed on the basis of historic cost but ignore pre-1982 inflation. The result, in most cases, is to produce a lower figure than that which results from basing the indexed rise on a deemed reacquisition in 1982.

Where the asset was acquired before 6 April 1965, the unindexed gain will normally be computed on the basis of a deemed reacquisition on 31 March 1982 (see chapter 8). But if this is not the case, part of the gain may be exempt under time apportionment. A difficult issue arises of whether time apportionment should be applied to the unindexed gain or after the indexation allowance has been deducted. The better view is that the latter is correct (cf CGTA 1979 Sch 5 para 11(2)).

Where the asset was acquired on a no gain/no loss disposal after 31 March 1982, the recipient is treated as having owned the asset on that date if the disponor or any previous no gain/no loss disponor so owned it (FA 1985 s.68(7), as amended by FA 1988 s.118). This enables the recipient's indexation allowance to be based on 1982 values and, to avoid double counting, the disponor's indexation allowance is not included in the recipient's acquisition cost. No gain/no loss disposal now bears the same meaning for these purposes as for 1982 rebasing (see p 44).

Special situations (FA 1982 Sch 13)

The apportionment of allowable expenditure required on a part disposal is effected before the indexation allowance is calculated. This means the indexed rises are calculated on the apportioned expenditure and not on the whole. The expenditure allocated to the retained part of the asset attracts the indexation allowance when the retained asset is disposed of.

Where a part disposal has been relieved by reducing the allowable expenditure attributable to the retained asset (see p 31), the indexation allowance on the retained asset is arrived at by first calculating the indexed rise on the unreduced expenditure. A calculation is then made of what the indexed rise would be on the reduction if it had been allowable expenditure. The real indexed rise is then reduced by this hypothetical indexed rise.

Acquisitions pursuant to a call option are treated as two separate items of expenditure. One consists of the money paid for the option, and this is treated as incurred when the option is granted. The other item is the money paid when the option is exercised, and this is incurred on the date of exercise.

Parallel pooling (FA 1985 Sch 19 paras 11-14)

Parallel pooling applies to new holdings. New holdings consist of shares and other poolable assets acquired after the 1982 date (see p 37). Disposals out of new holdings are not treated as part disposals for indexation purposes, and instead new holdings are subject to the special indexation rules, known as parallel pooling. As the name implies, parallel pooling involves keeping a pool of indexed expenditure in parallel with the pool of actual expenditure.

A new holding will have come into existence either on the 1985 date or, if the first acquisition was subsequent to that date, at the time of the first acquisition (see p 37). In the former event, the parallel pool is treated as coming into existence on the 1985 date and is the actual expenditure on the 1985 date plus the indexed rises that would have applied on the disposal of all the holding then. If the new holding comes into existence after the 1985 date, the initial parallel pool is simply the actual expenditure on that first acquisition.

The parallel pool is altered whenever the pool is added to or diminished. Any such event is known as an operative event, and it requires a calculation of the indexed rise in the pool, the RD month being the month of the operative event and the RI month the month of the last operative event or the coming into existence of the pool. This indexed rise is then added to the parallel pool and, if the operative event is an acquisition, so too is the actual cost of that acquisition.

On the disposal of the whole holding, the indexation allowance is simply the difference between the actual expenditure on the holding and the amount of the parallel pool. Where part of the holding is sold, the parallel pool is apportioned between the shares sold and the shares retained in the same proportions as the actual expenditure. The indexation allowance for the part sold is then the difference between the apportioned amounts of the expenditure and the parallel pool.

As with other assets, shares acquired under an option are subject to special rules. When the option is exercised, the option money and the cost of exercise go into the parallel pool in the normal way. But in addition, the parallel pool is also increased by the indexed rise on the option monies, RI being the month of grant, and RD the month of exercise.

Indexation

Example

During the 1980s Mr Jones made the following purchases and sales of ordinary shares in UK plc. He held no shares before 6 April 1982.

9 April 1983	Bought	2,000 for £2,200
14 July 1983	Bought	1,500 for £1,250
20 August 1985	Bought	1,200 for £2,000
15 December 1986	Sold	700 for £1,500
19 June 1987	Bought	800 for £1,700
5 March 1988	Sold	2,000 for £5,000

The retail prices index was as follows:

April 1983	332.5
July 1983	336.5
April 1985	373.9
October 1985	377.1
December 1986	378.9
June 1987	101.9 (following rebasing)
March 1988	104.1

Indexed rises are as follows:

RI April 1983/RD April 1985	0.125
RI July 1983/RD April 1985	0.111
RI April 1985/RD October 1985	0.009
RI October 1985/RD December 1986	0.42
RI December 1986/RD June 1987	.023
RI June 1987/RD March 1988	0.222

Qualifying expenditure and the indexed pool are calculated as follows:

	Shares	Qualifying expenditure £	Indexed pool £
April 1985	3,500	3,450	3,450
			275
			139
	3,500	3,450	3,864
October 1985 0.009 x 3,864			35
Purchase	1,200	2,000	2,000
	4,700	5,450	5,899
December 1986 0.042 x 5,899			248
	4,700	5,450	6,147

                                                            Unindexed assets

Sale	(700)	(812)	(916)
	4,000	4,638	5,231
June 1987			
.023 x 5,231			120
	4,000	4,638	5,351
Purchase	800	1,700	1,700
	4,800	6,338	7,051
March 1988			
.022 x 7,051			155
	4,800	6,338	7,206
Sale	(2,000)	(2,641)	(3,002)
	2,800	3,697	4,204

Unindexed assets

Certain assets do not enjoy an indexation allowance:
  (1) shares and securities disposed of within 10 days of aquisition (FA 1982 s.87(3)(a); FA 1985 Sch 19 para 18(4));
  (2) building society shares (FA 1988 s.113);
  (3) linked company debts on a security (FA 1988 Sch 11; see p 68).

III Chargeable Entities

Chapter 10

Individuals

Introduction (CGTA1979 s.2)

An individual is liable to capital gains tax for any year of assessment during which he is resident or ordinarily resident in the United Kingdom. Strictly the charge attaches to gains realised throughout the year even if he is only resident for part of the year. But by concession, disposals are not taxed if they are made before permanent residence begins or after it ceases (Concession D2). As with all concessions, this concession is not applied to facilitate artificial tax avoidance (cf *R v IRC, ex p Fulford-Dobson* [1987] STC 344).

The annual exemption (CGTA 1979 s.5)

Individuals are entitled to a basic annual exemption. This varies from year to year as it is subject to indexation. It has been held at the same level for 1988-9 and 1989-90 and stands at £5,000.

Each year, a calculation has to be made of the individual's taxable amount. This is the aggregate of his chargeable gains for the year as reduced by indexation, losses of the current year, and all other reliefs. Losses carried forward from previous years are also deducted, but only insofar as they do not cause the taxable amount to fall below the annual exemption for the year concerned. When the taxable amount has been arrived at, the annual exemption is deducted, and only the excess is liable to tax.

If an individual's gains are within the annual exemption and the proceeds of all disposals he has effected within the year are less than twice the exemption, he can enter a statement to that effect on his tax return. This discharges him from any obligation to give further details.

Individuals

Example 1
Mr Robinson makes disposals of chargeable assets in 1989-90 (when the exempt amount is £5,000) which produced:

Chargeable gains	£20,000
Allowable losses	£4,000

There were no allowable losses brought forward from 1988-89. The taxable amount for 1989-90 is £16,000 (£20,000-£4,000). The amount liable to tax is £11,000 (£16,000-£5,000).

Example 2
Mr Johnson has allowable losses brought forward of £2,000. In 1989-90 he realises chargeable gains of £4,000 and allowable losses of £2,200. The taxable amount for 1989-90 is:

Chargeable gains	£ 4,000
Deduct: Allowable losses	£ 2,200
Taxable amount	£ 1,800

As the taxable amount does not exceed £5,000 (exempt amount for 1989-90) Mr Johnson has no liability for tax in 1989-90. The allowable losses brought forward of £2,000 are not absorbed and can be carried forward to 1990-91.

Rates of tax (FA 1988 s.98)

Until 5 April 1988 the taxable gains of individuals were taxed at the flat rate of 30 per cent. This was changed by FA 1988, and now the rate of CGT is based on the individual's marginal rate of income tax.

The rate of tax for individuals whose total income is in excess of the higher-rate threshold is simply 40 per cent. Individuals whose total income and taxable gains are together within the basic-rate band pay tax at the basic rate (25 per cent) on their gains. Individuals whose income is within the basic-rate band but whose taxable gains take them over the higher rate threshold pay basic-rate tax on gains up to the threshold, and higher-rate tax on the balance.

Spouses: separate taxation (FA 1988 s.104)

From 6 April 1990, spouses will be treated as separate entities for capital gains tax purposes, in the same way as they will be for income tax. This means that the rate of tax on each spouse's gains will be determined solely by that spouse's income and gains, and each spouse will be entitled to a basic annual exemption. The only respect in which spouses will be treated as a single unit will be that disposals between them will be no gain/no loss disposals so long as they are living together (CGTA 1979 s.44).

Spouses: 1989-90 (CGTA 1979 ss.4, 44 and 45; FA 1988 s.99)

In 1989-90, spouses living together are treated as a single entity for CGT purposes. Accordingly they share the annual exemption in proportion to their taxable amounts, and the rate of tax on the wife's taxable gains is arrived at by treating them as the husband's gains. This means they must be aggregated with all his income and gains and with her investment income. They are also aggregated with her earnings unless the spouses have elected for separate taxation of the wife's earnings under TA 1988 s.287.

The basic rule in 1989-90 is that the husband is responsible for returning the wife's gains and for paying the tax attributable to them. But, as with income tax, either spouse may elect for tax to be assessed and recovered separately. Unfortunately this right of election is purely administrative, and does not prevent either the sharing of the exemption or the aggregation of the wife's gains in computing the rate of tax. An election must be made before 6 July next following the year to which it relates, but once made, it subsists until it is revoked.

In 1989-90, losses accruing to one spouse are deducted from gains accruing to the other, unless the spouses elect to the contrary. Disposals between spouses are no gain/no loss disposals, a situation which, as noted above, will continue after 5 April 1990.

Separation and divorce

It is to be noted that the relief for disposals between spouses requires them to be both married and living together. The better view is that it is lost once they are divorced but continues throughout the year assessment of any separation.

In 1989-90, the wife is entitled to a separate annual exemption for the year in which the spouses separate, but it applies only to gains realised after the separation. The husband's annual

Individuals

exemption has to be spread between his gains for the whole year and those of his wife prior to separation.

The same principles apply in 1989-90 in determining the rate of tax on the wife's gains. Net gains accruing prior to the separation are aggregated with the husband's income and gains, but gains accruing thereafter are taxed solely on the basis of the wife's marginal rate of income tax (FA 1988 s.99(4)).

Partners (CGTA 1979 s.60)

Partnerships are not separate entities for CGT purposes. Instead dealings by the firm are treated as dealings by the individual partners, and the partners individually are assessable and chargeable with any tax due. It is to be inferred from this that, for CGT purposes, each partner is treated as the absolute owner of a fractional share of each partnership asset.

In practice the CGT treatment of partnerships is governed by the well-known Statement of Practice issued by the Revenue in 1975 (SP D12). The main points are as follows:

1. The size of each partner's fractional share in the partnership assets is determined by his share in asset surpluses or, if this is not laid down, by his general profit share.
2. The value of each partner's share is the appropriate fraction of the total value of the asset, and is not discounted.
3. When a partner withdraws an asset in specie from the partnership, the other partners' shares are disposed of at market value. The acquiring partner's share of the gain is carried forward and deducted from his acquisition cost.
4. Changes in profit-sharing ratios, including the introduction or retirement of a partner, do not result in a chargeable gain unless either the assets have been revalued in the partnership accounts or payment is made outside the accounts. The fractional shares of each partner are simply increased or diminished on a no gain/no loss basis.
5. Market value is not substituted on transactions between partners on arm's length terms. This is so even if the partners are connected otherwise than as partners.
6. A retirement annuity paid to a retiring partner is not treated as consideration for the disposal of his share in the partnership assets unless it exceeds reasonable recognition of his past contribution to the partnership.

One point not covered by the 1975 statement was the position where a partnership is dissolved and the assets are divided in specie. The Revenue view in these circumstances is that each partner disposes of his fractional share in all the assets taken by the other partners (see point (3) above). This view, however, may not be consistent with *Jenkins v Brown* [1989] STC 577, where it was decided that a partition of jointly held land did not occasion any disposals. But if the Revenue view is accepted, partners who use the assets they take in a new business may in practice claim roll-over relief (ESC D23).

Changes in sharing ratios are treated as no gain/no loss disposals for the purposes of 1982 rebasing and indexation (SP 1/89). This extension of the 1975 statement was necessary because changes in sharing ratios are not included in the statutory lists of no gain/no loss disposals. Without the extension, partnershp changes would progressively cause partnerships to lose the benefits of rebasing, for the partners disposing of the assets held since 1982 would come to be different from the partners in 1982 and yet their acquisition cost would the original acquisition cost.

Chapter 11

Companies

General (TA 1988 ss.6, 13 and 345)

Companies do not pay capital gains tax as such. Instead the chargeable gains and allowable losses of each accounting period are aggregated, and, if the resultant figure is a gain, that gain is included in full in the company's chargeable profits.

Gains and losses are computed in accordance with the same rules as apply for CGT proper. As with CGT, losses can be relieved against the gains of the current accounting period, and, insofar as not so relieved, against the gains of future accounting periods. Indexation applies fully to companies, but there is no equivalent of the basic annual exemption.

Although in substance both corporate and non-corporate net gains are taxed as income, the form differs. Corporate gains are actually included in chargeable profits, and accordingly may be reduced by trading losses of the same and the succeeding accounting period and by charges on income and management expenses. Non-corporate gains, by contrast, are still subject to a separate tax, and so cannot be reduced by any income relief.

In one respect, the assimilation of corporate gains with income profits is incomplete. If a company has net losses rather than net gains, those losses can only be relieved by being carried forward against future gains. They cannot be relieved against income profits of the same accounting period.

Small companies and ACT

For many years, net gains did not qualify for the small companies' rate of corporation tax and gains could not be taken into account in determining the extent to which ACT could be set against mainstream corporation tax. Both these restrictions were abolished in 1987. The position now is that taxable gains are taken into account in determining whether the small companies' rate applies, and they are themselves taxed at the rate. So too, the maximum ACT which may be set against mainstream tax is the ACT that would have been chargeable if the distributions for the period, plus ACT thereon, equalled both the income profits and the net gains of the period.

For 1989-90, the small companies rate is 25 per cent and it is payable if the company's profits, and those of any associated company are below £150,000 (TA 1988 s.13; FA 1989 s.35). Marginal relief applies on profits up to £750,000. The ACT rate is 1/3, which equals tax at the basic rate on the grossed up amount of the dividend (TA 1988 s.14).

Where a small company is a closely held investment company the small companies rate is not available. This means that both income and capital profits attract the main rate of corporation tax (TA 1988 s.13A as inserted by FA 1989 s.105).

Liquidation (TA 1988 s.345; CGTA 1979 s.72)

Assets vested in the liquidator are treated for tax purposes as belonging to the company, and disposals and acquistions between the liquidator and the company are disregarded. As a result, the winding-up of a company does not of itself trigger any disposal of the company's assets.

Disposals do occur when the liquidator in fact realises assets or when he effects a distribution in specie to the shareholders. Distributions of the latter kind are deemed to take place at market value (CGTA 1979 s.29A).

The shareholder does not suffer any form of deemed disposal of his shares when the company goes into liquidation, but instead he is treated as making a part disposal whenever he receives a distribution. The application of the part disposal formula (see p 31) means that by the time the disribution of assets is completed, no allowable expenditure is left to be attributed to the shares.

Double taxation

It is inherent in the tax treatment of companies that corporate gains are taxed twice before the proceeds reach the shareholders. The first charge is on the company when it effects the disposal and, as just noted, the gain is fully liable to corporation tax. The second charge arises either when the company distributes the gain by way of dividend or when the shareholder sells his

Companies

shares or receives a distribution on the liquidation of the company. In the former case, the charge is to higher-rate income tax, and this charge is only avoided if the shareholder is not a higher-rate taxpayer. Otherwise the tax to consider is CGT, and this will be charged on the basis of values inflated by the net corporate gain.

Groups (TA 1970 s.272 as amended by FA 1989 s.138)

Groups of companies are subject to several special provisions in the CGT code. They are not, however, treated as one for CGT purposes. Accordingly there is no aggregation of group gains and group losses to give an aggregate gain or loss for the group as a whole. Similarly the losses of one group member cannot be relieved against the gains of another: they can only be relieved against the future gains of the company to which they accrued.

Until 14 March 1989 a group for CGT purposes meant a parent company and its 75 per cent subsidiaries. A company is a 75 per cent subsidiary if the parent is the beneficial owner of 75 per cent of its ordinary share capital. The ownership can be direct or through other subsidiaries and ordinary share capital is all share capital other than that whose holders are entitled only to a dividend at a fixed rate (TA 1988 ss.832 and 838).

Since 14 March 1989 it has remained the position that a company is not included in a group unless it is a 75 per cent subsidiary of the parent. But in addition a further test must be satisfied. The parent must be beneficially entitled to more than 50 per cent of both any profits available for distribution during the life of the company and any assets available for distribution if the company is wound up.

A company is not treated as leaving a group if it would only do so because it or some other company is wound up. Where the parent of one group joins another group, the two groups are regarded as the same.

Intra group disposals (TA 1970 ss.273 and 278)

One important relief available to groups of companies is that disposals between member companies of a group are no gain/no loss disposals. This means that any gain which would otherwise accrue is automatically held over to the recipient company. As with most no gain/no loss disposals, if the disponor company held the asset on 31 March 1982, the recipient is treated as having held it then and can compute its indexation allowance accordingly (FA 1985 s.68(7); FA 1988 Sch 8 para 1).

The relief for intra group disposals can be effectively used to relieve losses against group gains. If company A has accumulated capital losses and company B is about to realise a gain on an outside disposal, company B can first transfer the asset to company A. That transfer will be a no gain/no loss disposal and so the gain will accrue on the outside disposal by company A, when it can be offset against company A's losses.

In law such an exercise of this kind is capable of coming within the *Ramsay* principle if negotiations for the outside disposal have largely been concluded. But in practice the Revenue have confirmed that they will not normally invoke the principle provided the company with the losses was in the group when the losses arose (ICAEW, Guidance Note TR 588, reproduced [1985] STI 568). One potential drawback is that roll-over relief may be lost, for entitlement to that relief depends on how the asset is used by the final group member to own it. Law and practice in this area are discussed on pp 118–9.

The relief for disposals between group members can be clawed back if the recipient company leaves the group at any time within the following six years (TA 1970 s.278). Such a departure triggers a deemed disposal if the departing company has retained the asset or if it has disposed of it and made a roll-over claim in respect of a new asset. The disposal is treated as taking place at the time of the no gain/no loss disposal at the then market value of the asset. Any tax due may be recovered from the parent.

Groups and 1982 rebasing (FA 1988 Sch 8 paras 13 and 14)

An election for 1982 rebasing to apply to all the taxpayer's assets cannot be made by each company in a group. One election only can be made and, once made, it binds all members of the group. The election must be made by the parent before 6 April 1990 or within two years of the accounting period in which a group member first disposes of an asset owned since 31 March 1982.

Special rules govern the application of an election or non-election to companies leaving or joining a group. As a result of these rules it is possible for a group to include a company not covered by the group election or non-election. If an intra-group transfer after 5 April 1988 involves such a company, the asset concerned is governed by the election or non-election applicable to the disponor group member rather than the recipient (FA 1988 Sch 8 para 2).

Companies

Group avoidance

Groups of companies could in the absence of special provisions use the indexation allowance to create losses on loans within the group. Such loans count as chargeable assets so long as the debt is on a security (see p 87) and provided they are retained within the group, they are not exempt as qualifying corporate bonds (see p 86). It is inherent in such loans that they do not in fact increase in value, and accordingly, application of the indexation allowance would result in a loss.

Exercises of this kind were countered in 1988 by withdrawing the indexation allowance from linked debts on a security (FA 1988 Sch 11). These are debts between what are called linked companies. The latter are companies which are grouped or associated, 'group' for these purposes meaning a parent and its 51 per cent subsidiaries. If two companies become linked after the debt was created, the allowance is only made in respect of inflation prior to linking.

The 1988 legislation also deals with redeemable preference shares held by one linked company in another and requires the indexation allowance to be reduced by a just and reasonable amount. Similar provisions apply to ordinary shares held by one linked company in another if their acquisition was funded by a third linked company.

Another form of group avoidance occurs when the parent reduces the value of a subsidiary by causing it to pay a substantial dividend or transfer assets to another group member at an undervalue. Such dividends and transfers are not taxable (TA 1970 s.273; TA 1988 s.208). If the subsidiary is subsequently disposed of, the effect of such exercises is to avoid CGT, for they reduce the value of the subsidiary and thus any gain.

Prima facie such exercises should be caught and counteracted by the value shifting rules in CGTA 1979 s.26 (see p 24). In fact until 14 March 1989 s.26 was specifically prevented from applying. Since that date it has been able to apply, but only in very limited circumstances. A dividend only causes s.26 to apply if it is paid out of profits attributable to an asset which (a) was not disposed of out of the group; and (b) leaves the group with the subsidiary. A transfer at an undervalue is only caught if it is tainted by tax avoidance and the actual consideration is less than cost.

Dividends and transfers at an undervalue can also be caught by TA 1970 ss.280 and 281. These sections only apply if the subsidiary is disposed of at a loss, but subject to that, their application is not restricted in the way in which s.26 is. Where

Unit trusts (CGTA 1979 ss.92 and 93; FA 1980 s.81)

they apply, the loss is reduced by such amount as appears to the Revenue just and reasonable.

Unit trusts (CGTA 1979 ss.92 and 93; FA 1980 s.81)

For capital gains tax purposes, the term 'unit trust scheme' has since 11 March 1988 had the meaning given to it in the Financial Services Act 1986. The term 'authorised unit trust' is given the same definition as it has for income tax purposes. It is any unit trust scheme approved under the Financial Services Act 1986 s.78 (TA 1988 s.468).

Since February 1988 the Revenue have had power to make regulations to exclude what would otherwise be unit trust schemes from being such schemes for CGT purposes. This regulation-making power has a comparable income tax equivalent in TA 1988 s.469(7). It is exercisable by statutory instrument. So far this power has only been exercised for CGT purposes in favour of limited partnerships and approved profit-sharing schemes.

For capital gains tax purposes all unit trust schemes (unless excluded by the regulations just mentioned) count as companies, and the rights of the unit-holders as shares. Potentially this means that unit trust schemes, like companies, are subject to double taxation, once when the trustees realise investments and again when the unit-holders dispose of their units. However this double taxation is subject to two important reliefs:

(1) the gains of authorised unit trusts are not taxable;
(2) the gains of any unit trust for exempt unit holders are also exempt. Unit trusts for exempt holders are unit trusts set up to handle the investments of charities and other persons exempt from capital gains tax and corporation tax.

Chapter 12

Trusts and Settlements

Introduction

The CGT legislation draws a distinction between settled property and nominee property. The categories are mutually exclusive, in that settled property is defined as all property vested in trustees which is not nominee property. The significance of the distinction is that nominee property is treated as belonging to the beneficial owner whereas the trustees of settled property are treated as a separate entity. The term 'nominee property' is not used in the legislation but was coined by Goulding J in *Booth v Ellard* [1978] STC 487 and has passed into general use.

The definition of settled property (CGTA 1979 s.46)

As just noted, settled property is all property vested in trustees which is not nominee property. Property is nominee property if it is held either for:

(a) a person absolutely entitled as against the trustee, or
(b) a person who would be absolutely entitled as against the trustee but for being an infant or under a disability, or
(c) two or more persons who are or would be jointly so entitled.

The phrase 'absolutely entitled' is at the heart of this definition. The legislation provides that a person is absolutely entitled as against the trustee if he has the exclusive right to direct how the property is dealt with, subject only to the trustee's right to resort to the property for taxes, costs, and other outgoings.

Case law has fleshed out this definition and the following points are now established:

(a) Two or more persons are only absolutely entitled if their interests are concurrent — ie they are joint tenants or tenants in common. If their interests are successive, as where they are life tenant and remainderman, the property is settled

The trustees of settled property (CGTA 1979 s.52)

property even if all beneficiaries are sui juris and able to terminate the trust (*Kidson v Macdonald* [1974] STC 54; *Stephenson v Barclays Bank Trust Co Ltd* [1975] STC 151).
(b) One set of trustees may be absolutely entitled as against another set of trustees (*Roome v Edwards* [1981] STC 96; *Bond v Pickford* [1983] STC 517). Typically this happens where trust property is vested in nominees or where fiduciary powers are exercised so as to create a new settlement.
(c) An infant is only absolutely entitled to property if his interest is vested and indefeasible and so forms part of his estate if he dies. If his entitlement is subject to his attaining a specified age, the property is settled property (*Tomlinson v Glyns Executor and Trustee Co* [1970] 1 All ER 381).

As a result of these and other cases, it is now clear that the term 'settled property' comprehends all property held in what are generally regarded as settlements. Thus strict settlements, interest in possession trusts, accumulation and maintenance trusts, and discretionary trusts are all settlements for CGT purposes.

The trustees of settled property (CGTA 1979 s.52)

The trustees of settled property are treated as a single continuing body of persons. They are thus a separate entity and changes in the trusteeship are disregarded. In contrast to income tax, trustees are so treated regardless of whether the trust is discretionary or fixed interest. If the settlement is a strict settlement, the single continuing body includes the life tenant.

The single body represented by the trustees is treated as resident in the UK unless all or a majority of the trustees are non-resident and the general administration of the trusts is carried on abroad. A trustee is treated as non-resident if the settlor was non-resident and non-domiciled when he made the settlement and the trustee carries on the business of managing trusts. This protects the position of trust corporations attracting foreign trust business to the UK and if all or a majority of the trustees of such a trust are or are treated as non-resident, the administration of the trusts is deemed to be carried on abroad.

Although the trustees are a single body, the Revenue are empowered to assess and recover tax from any one of the trustees. It is no defence for a trustee that he has never controlled the asset disposed of or received the proceeds of its sale (*Roome v Edwards* [1981] STC 96).

Trusts and settlements

Actual and deemed disposals (CGTA 1979 ss.53-6)

Property transferred into a settlement is deemed to be disposed of by the settlor to the trustees at market value. This is so regardless of whether the settlor is a beneficiary or even the life tenant under the settlement. Any gain may be held over if the trustees are resident and either the trust is discretionary or the assets settled are business assets (see chapter 18).

When the trustees realise investments, any gains and losses are computed in the same way as for other taxpayers. The indexation allowance is available and losses may be set against the gains of the current and future years.

Should the trust be an interest in possession trust the death of the life tenant occasions a deemed disposal of the trust assets at market value. But in accordance with the general relief applying on death, no chargeable gain accrues save to the extent that any such gain represents a gain previously held over on the transfer of the asset concerned into the settlement. This exemption on the death of the life tenant applies both if the settlement continues or if it comes to an end by reason of another beneficiary becoming absolutely entitled.

A deemed disposal also occurs if a beneficiary becomes absolutely entitled to settled property otherwise than on the death of the life tenant. Here any gain accruing is chargeable, although it may be held over if the beneficiary is UK resident and either the trust is an accumulation and maintenance trust or the assets the beneficiary receives are business assets (see chapter 18).

Since one set of trustees can be absolutely entitled as against another set of trustees, a deemed disposal can occur even if the property remains settled. But a deemed disposal of this kind only occurs if the trustees of the first settlement have power to advance or resettle the trust property and exercise that power by creating a new settlement or by transferring the property to the trustees of a second pre-existing settlement (*Roome v Edwards* [1981] STC 96; *Bond v Pickford* [1983] STC 517). If the trustees of the first settlement can revoke the second settlement, or if its trusts are non-exhaustive, the property is treated as remaining in the first settlement and no deemed disposal occurs (SP 7/84).

The basic annual exemption (CGTA 1979 Sch 1)

Trustees of settled property are entitled to an annual exemption but it is equal to only half the exempt amount available to individuals, and so now stands at £2,500 (CGTA 1979 Sch 1 para 6).

Attribution of gains to the settlor (FA 1988 Sch 10)

The exemption is subject to a further restriction if the trust was made after 6 June 1978. It is necessary to count the number of settlements made by the same settlor since that date, and the exemption for each is half the exempt amount divided by the number of the settlements. If there are more than five settlements each is entitled to a minimum exemption of one tenth of the exempt amount (currently £500).

An annual exemption equal to the exempt amount for individuals is available for two forms of trust, namely trusts for the mentally handicapped and trusts for persons in receipt of an attendance allowance. A trust falls within these categories if half any income and capital paid out is paid out to or for the benefit of the disabled person

Rates of tax (FA 1988 s.100)

Until 5 April 1988 the taxable gains of all trusts were charged at the same rate as those of individuals, namely 30 per cent. But now this has changed and different rates of tax apply to different kinds of trust.

A distinction has to be drawn between trusts whose income is liable to the additional rate under TA 1988 s.686 and trusts whose income is not so liable. In broad terms, the additional rate is applicable where the trust income has to be accumulated or paid out at the discretion of the trustees. It is not applicable to fixed-interest trusts, where the life tenant is entitled to the income as of right and it is taxed as his.

If the trust is a fixed-interest trust, the rate of CGT is equal to the basic rate of income tax, currently 25 per cent. The rate of tax on accumulation and discretionary trusts is equal to the basic rate plus the additional rate, currently 35 per cent.

A trap exists where part of a settlement is subject to discretionary or accumulation trusts and part to fixed-interest trusts. Here it is generally thought that the 35 per cent rate applies to the fixed-interest fund as well as to the rest of the settlement. The only way in which the 25 per cent rate can be secured is to ensure that throughout the year of assessment the entire settlement is subject to fixed-interest trusts.

Attribution of gains to the settlor (FA 1988 Sch 10)

Certain settlements do not qualify either for the 25 or 35 per cent rates of tax or for a basic annual exemption. Instead the trust gains for each year are added together, and, after deducting any allowable losses, the net gain is treated as accruing to the settlor. It is taxed in his hands at his marginal rate of income tax, credit being given for his annual exemption to the extent that the latter is otherwise unutilised.

Settlements treated in this way are settlements in which the settlor has an interest. The settlor may have an interest either because of the terms of the trust or on account of the way in which the trust fund is dealt with. He is caught under the terms of the trust if he or his spouse are actual or potential beneficiaries. He is caught by what happens in practice if he or his spouse enjoy a benefit from the trust fund.

These provisions are the CGT equivalent of the income tax legislation which attributes income to the settlor if he is a beneficiary or receives a capital sum (TA 1988 ss.672-4 and 677). As with that legislation, the provisions are excluded in certain instances, notably where the settlor only takes on the failure of a beneficiary to attain 25. The provisions do not apply if either the settlor or the trust is non-resident, and the settlor has a right to recover any tax he pays from the trustees.

Beneficial interests (CGTA 1979 s.58)

A beneficial interest under a settlement is an asset just as much as any other form of property. Its value is determined by the terms of the settlement, and, while revocable interests or interests under protective or discretionary trusts are worthless, vested life interests and reversions can have substantial value.

For CGT purposes, the original beneficiary has no acquisition cost, for there is no corresponding disposal (CGTA 1979 s.29A; see p 17). When the original beneficiary or an assignee becomes absolutely entitled to the settled property two disposals occur, namely a disposal of the trust assets at market value by the trustees and a disposal of the beneficial interest by the beneficiary. This latter disposal is treated as taking place at the value of the assets to which the beneficiary becomes entitled (CGTA 1979 s.58(2)). In the absence of relieving provisions these rules would result in substantial double taxation.

In fact, in most cases these consequences are avoided for beneficial interests are not chargeable assets unless (a) the holder of the interest has bought it or (b) the settlement is non-resident. In the latter case, the interest is only partially chargeable, for while an assignment is chargeable, the occasion on which the beneficiary becomes absolutely entitled is not. Should a resident

Beneficial interests (CGTA 1979 s.58)

settlement become non-resident, any previous disposal of a beneficial interest becomes assessable on the trustees unless in the meantime all the trust assets have been disposed of (FA 1981 s.88; see p 135).

IV Exemptions

Chapter 13

Private Residences

Exempt property (CGTA 1979 s.101)

A private dwelling-house is exempt if it has been the taxpayer's only or main residence throughout his ownership or since 31 March 1982 (FA 1988 Sch 8 para 8). The exemption takes in flats and maisonettes as well as houses, for in law these are dwelling-houses and the exemption is in any event expressed as applying to parts of dwelling-houses. It also embraces the interests of co-owners, for it applies to interests in dwelling-houses as much as to dwellings as a whole.

In the normal case, the taxpayer's dwelling-house is a single building. But it is now established that a dwelling may include staff accommodation, stabling and garages, and in appropriate cases these may be physically separate from the house proper (*Batey v Wakefield* [1981] STC 521). But it is a question of fact as to whether a physically distinct building is in fact part of the dwelling-house for these purposes (*Markey v Sanders* [1987] STC 256; *Williams v Merrylees* [1987] STC 445).

The exemption is not expressly applied to caravans and houseboats. But a permanently sited caravan can count as a dwelling-house if it is attached to main services (*Makins v Elson* [1977] STC 46; *Moore v Thompson* [1986] STC 170).

Two or more residences (CGTA 1979 s.101)

If a taxpayer has two homes, the exemption only applies to his main residence. He can choose which his main residence is, but the right of election is prospective. Notice of the election has to be given to the Inspector within two years of the beginning of the period to which it relates. A notice can be revoked, but again only for a period starting not earlier than two years before the notice of revocation.

Private residences

If an election has not been made, the question of which home is the taxpayer's main residence is determined as one of fact. Initially the determination is made by the Inspector, but the taxpayer has a right of appeal to the Commissioners. Even on this objective test the taxpayer's main residence is not necessarily the one where he spends the most time. Thus in *Frost v Feltham* [1981] STC 115, a publican's main residence was held to be a cottage he visited a few times each month.

Spouses are only entitled to the exemption in respect of one residence between them. This will remain so even after married couples are taxed separately in 1990. If the husband owns one house and the wife the other, both have to sign an election choosing one as their main residence.

It is particularly important to make an election where one residence is freehold and the other is occupied under a rack-rent tenancy of negligible value. The latter counts as residence just as much as the former and if on the facts it is the main residence, failure to make an election will have unfortunate CGT consequences. The Revenue do allow a late election to be made, but only if the taxpayer has been unaware that one was required (Extra Statutory Concession D21).

Periods of absence (CGTA 1979 s.102)

The basic rule is that a dwelling-house is only fully exempt if it has been the taxpayer's only or main residence throughout his ownership or, if it was acquired before 31 March 1982, since then. But certain periods of absence count as residence and if even with them included, the house was not the taxpayers's only or main residence for all the necessary period, a proportionate part of any gain is relieved.

The first period of absence to count as residence is the last two years of ownership. This protects the position of the taxpayer who has to move before he has been able to sell his house. In practice a corresponding period of deemed residence is allowed at the beginning of a taxpayer's ownership if he is unable to move in on account of building works (Inland Revenue Statement of Practice D4).

Next a taxpayer is allowed to treat any period during which he is living in job-related accommodation as a period of residence. Job-related accommodation bears the same meaning as for mortgage interest relief purposes (TA 1988 s.356). In broad terms it is accommodation provided by reason of the taxpayer's employment which is either (a) necessary for the proper

Periods of absence (CGTA 1979 s.102)

performance of his duties or (b) customarily provided for the employment or (c) provided for security reasons. If the taxpayer does live in job-related accommodation, any residence he owns is only treated as *a* residence, and so an election may be needed to make it his main residence.

Finally three specific periods of absence count as residence. They are (a) any period not exceeding three years, (b) any period not exceeding four years when the taxpayer has to live elsewhere because of his employment, and (c) any period of whatever length during which the taxpayer is employed abroad. Strictly, the taxpayer has to be in actual occupation of the residence both before and after any of these three periods. But in practice this condition may be relaxed after the second and third kinds of absence if the terms of the taxpayer's employment require him to work elsewhere (Extra Statutory Concession D4).

If after all these rules have been applied, the residence is not or is not deemed to have been the taxpayer's only or main residence throughout his ownership or since 31 March 1982 any gain is apportioned. The apportionment is done with reference to a fraction, of which the numerator is the period of actual or deemed residence since 31 March 1982 and the denominator the period of ownership or the period since 31 March 1982.

Example
Mr Smith bought a London house on 17 May 1980. He occupied it as his main residence until 30 June 1983, when he moved to the Isle of Wight and elected for a bungalow there to be treated as his main residence. He sold the London house on 30 June 1988 and realised an indexed gain of £100,000.

Period of ownership:	
1 April 1982–30 June 1988	75 months
Period of occupation	
Actual: 1 April 82–30 June 88	15 months
Notional: 30 June 86–30 June 88	24 months
	39 months
Exempt gain $\frac{39}{75}$ x £100,000	£52,000
Chargeable gain $\frac{36}{75}$ x £100,000	£48,000

Private residences

A quirk in the legislation favours taxpayers whose sole period of residence was before 31 March 1982. One would have thought that such taxpayers would not qualify for the relief at all, for there is no period of actual residence after 1982. In fact however, they can count the last 24 months of ownership as a period of residence (CGTA 1979 ss.101(5) and 102(4)). Accordingly, a taxpayer who disposes of such a residence on 5 April 1990 attracts relief on one quarter of the gain.

Lettings (FA 1980 s.80)

The private residence exemption is not jeopardised if the house is let during the periods of absence which count as residence. In practice it is not jeopardised either if the taxpayer lets rooms in the house, provided the taxpayer and the occupants of the rooms live as one household and take meals together (SP 14/80).

In other circumstances, lettings do cause partial loss of the exemption. If a letting is of the whole house, the period of the letting is ipso facto a period of non-residence and the fraction described above has to be applied. But where the letting is of part only of the house, the part of the gain which loses the exemption is arrived at by multiplying the gain by two fractions. The first is the fraction of the house which is let and second the fraction of the period of ownership during which it is let.

If as a result of these rules the letting has prevented part of the gain from attracting the exemption all may not be lost. A further relief, conferred by FA 1980 s.80, comes into play. This applies if (a) part of the gain qualifies for the private residence exemption proper and (b) the house has at any time been let as residential accommodation. Where these conditions are satisfied, the gain otherwise chargeable is exempt to the extent that it does not exceed the lesser of £20,000 and the gain qualifying for private residence relief proper.

Section 80 is an important and often overlooked section. It should be remembered that it can apply as much where the whole house is let as where part of it is let, and it even comes into operation if the house is bought tenanted and subsequently occupied by the owner. It only applies if the letting is a letting to people who are likely to use the accommodation as their home: the relief is not available to hoteliers or boarding house keepers (*Owen v Elliott* [1989] STC 44).

Business use (CGTA 1979 s.103)

Exclusive business use of part of a house causes the private residence exemption to be lost in respect of that part. Obvious examples are a doctor's surgery or a shop occupying the ground floor of the house. But the exemption is not jeopardised if the business use is non-exclusive, involving for example a study, for a study is an integral part of many houses. Self-employed taxpayers who claim a proportion of the running costs of their home as a business expense do not lose relief either, at least so long as no part of the house is used exclusively for business.

Garden and grounds (CGTA 1979 s.101(2)-(4))

The garden or grounds of a house qualify for the private residence exemption insofar as they do not exceed the permitted area. This is one acre (inclusive of the house) or such large area as is required for the reasonable enjoyment of the house as a residence. If the grounds exceed the permitted area, the exemption applies to the part most suitable for occupation and enjoyment with the house.

In cases where the garden or grounds exceed one acre, the question of what is required for the reasonable enjoyment of the house is one of fact for the Commissioners. The test is objective, so a taxpayer with a propensity for horticulture who occupies a small cottage will almost certainly be restricted to an acre, but the taxpayer occupying a substantial mansion may secure the exemption for a considerable area. If the dwelling-house includes stabling it may be possible to argue that a paddock should be included in the permitted area, since it is required for the horses to graze in.

In law it is essential to sell the garden or grounds at the same time as or before the house proper, for once the taxpayer ceases to own the house, the exemption ceases to apply to the garden (*Varty v Lynes* [1976] STC 508). But in practice the Revenue do not take the point unless the garden has development value (FRP B/25). If the garden exceeds one acre and part is sold before the house, it may be difficult to secure the exemption on that part, for the sale is ipso facto evidence that the land sold is not required for the reasonable enjoyment of the house.

Private residences

Settled property (CGTA 1979 s.104)

A dwelling-house held in trust qualifies for the private residence exemption if it is the only or main residence of a beneficiary entitled to occupy it under the terms of the settlement. A beneficiary is so entitled if the settlement gives him the right to occupy the house or if the trustees allow him into occupation in exercise of an expressly conferred power (*Varty v Lynes* [1976] STC 494). Such powers are now inserted in most settlements, and so the practical position is that the private residence exemption is capable of applying to residences held in most forms of trust.

Should the trust residence be only one of the beneficiary's residences the notice of election has to be signed by both the trustees and the beneficiary. Discretionary trustees who allow a beneficiary into occupation should remember that they may be treated for inheritance tax purposes as giving him an interest in possession. This could result in an exit charge (see further SP 10/79).

Dependent relatives (CGTA 1979 s.105)

Before 6 April 1988, dwellings occupied by dependent relatives of the taxpayer attracted the private residence exemption. Taxpayers could only claim this additional relief in respect of one property, or, in the cases of spouses, one property between them. The term 'dependent relative' was defined as (a) the taxpayer's mother if she was widowed, divorced or separated, or (b) any other relation incapacitated by old age or infirmity from maintaining himself. To attract the relief, the property had to be the sole residence of the relative and provided rent-free and without other consideration.

The dependent relative relief now only applies in limited circumstances (FA 1988 s.111). It is only available if the conditions for the relief were satisfied at some time between 31 March 1982 and 5 April 1988. If they continue to be satisfied by the same relative at all times thereafter until the residence is sold, relief is available in full. But if the dependent relative in occupation before 6 April 1988 has ceased to occupy the property, whether before or after 6 April, then only the proportion of the gain attributable to his pre-1988 occupation is exempt.

Anti-avoidance (CGTA 1979 s.103(3))

The private residence exemption is not available to a taxpayer who acquires a house with a view to realising a gain from its disposal. It does not apply also to any gain attributable to enhancement expenditure incurred with a view to realising a gain. These rules are rarely invoked by the Revenue in practice, but they should be kept in mind by the taxpayers wanting to take undue advantage of the private residence relief.

Chapter 14

Exempt Intangibles

Gilts (CGTA 1979 s.67)

Gilt-edged securities are exempt from CGT. This apparently relieving provision is not such at all, for indexation means that if gilts were chargeable, they would mostly generate allowable losses. At one time gilts were not exempt if the taxpayer had owned them for less than a year, but this rule was abolished with effect from 2 July 1986.

A complete list of gilt-edged securities is given in CGTA 1979 Sch 2, as updated by subsequent statutory instruments. The exemption for gilts applies also to futures and options in gilts.

Qualifying corporate bonds (CGTA 1979 s.67; FA 1984 s.64)

Qualifying corporate bonds are exempt from CGT. As with gilts, this is not really an exemption, for indexation means that chargeable gains would rarely accrue on the disposal of qualifying corporate bonds. The exemption is extended to futures and options in qualifying corporate bonds.

A bond counts as a qualifying corporate bond if it satisfies the following conditions:

(1) It must be a security for the purposes of CGTA 1979 s.82. That section provides that a security for these purposes can be secured or unsecured. The term includes loan stock or a similar security issued by one of the following:-
   (a) the UK or any other government;
   (b) any public or local authority in the UK or elsewhere;
   (c) any company.
(2) The debt which the security represents must be a normal commercial loan. The definition of this term is complex, but in essence the loan must be non-convertible and carry a commercial rate of interest which is not dependent on the results of the borrower's business (TA 1988 Sch 18).

Debts (CGTA 1979 s.134)

(3) The loan must be denominated in sterling and must not be capable of conversion into any other currency.
(4) The bond must have been issued or acquired after 13 March 1984.

Originally a bond was only a qualifying corporate bond if it or the company which issued it were quoted. This requirement has been removed as respects disposals taking place on or after 14 March 1989 (FA 1989 s.139(2)). The term has also been extended to include securities which count as deep gain securities for the purposes of FA 1989 Sch 11 (FA 1989 s.139(3)). A bond is not a qualifying corporate bond if it was issued by one group member to another, but such a bond becomes a qualifying coporate bond if and for so long as it is owned by a non group member (FA 1984 s.64(7) as amended by FA 1989 s.139(5)).

Debts (CGTA 1979 s.134)

For CGT purposes a debt is treated as an asset of the creditor and this asset is disposed of either when the creditor assigns the debt or when the debtor repays it. A debt is exempt unless either:

(1) it belongs to a person other than the original creditor; or
(2) it is a debt on a security.

The term 'debt on a security' is one which has troubled the courts, for it has no recognised meaning. Security has the same meaning as in the definition of qualifying corporate bond, but this definition is only inclusive. It is reasonably plain that a debt can only be a debt on a security if it is a corporate or institutional debt. But not all corporate debts are debts on a security, for an ordinary loan to a company results in a simple debt and no more (*Aberdeen Construction Group Ltd v IRC* [1978] STC 127). To be a debt on a security a debt must be a contractual loan with a structure of permanence. It need not be constituted by a document but it must be capable of being dealt in at a profit (*W T Ramsay Ltd v IRC* [1982] AC 300).

In almost all cases the exemption of simple debts prevents losses from being allowable rather than gains chargeable. But in one situation an original creditor who suffers a loss on a debt may claim an allowable loss. This is possible if the following conditions are satisfied (CGTA 1979 s.136):

(a) the borrower is a trader who used the borrowed money for the purposes of his business;

Exempt intangibles

(b) the borrower is UK resident; and
(c) the loan has become irrecoverable.

Foreign currency bank accounts (CGTA 1979 s.135)

In law a bank account is a debt owed by the banker to the customer. The basic CGT rule is that the general exemption for debts does not apply to foreign currency bank accounts and accordingly a disposal occurs whenever money is withdrawn from a foreign currency account or switched between accounts. Gains and losses accrue equal to the difference in the sterling exchange rate of the currency when the deposit was made and the sterling exchange rate at the time of the withdrawal.

One statutory relief applies. A foreign currency account is exempt from CGT if it represents currency acquired for the personal expenditure abroad of the taxpayer and his family. Personal expenditure for these purposes includes the provision or maintenance of a foreign home. This exemption also applies to foreign currency held in specie (CGTA 1979 s.133).

In practice a further relief is also available for foreign accounts in that a taxpayer may treat all accounts in his name in any given currency as single asset (SP 10/84). The effect of this is to prevent transfers between the accounts from being a disposal, although disposals do still occur once the taxpayer switches into another currency or draws out cash.

Damages

As noted in chapters 2 and 3, a right of an action is an asset (*Zim Properties Ltd v Proctor* [1985] STC 90). Sums awarded in damages or paid to settle the action count as capital sums derived from this asset and so are liable to CGT.

This poses serious problems in law, because normally a right of action has no acquisition cost. Market value cannot be substituted, because there is no corresponding disposal (see chapter 4). Accordingly, in law damages or sums paid to compromise the action are generally liable to CGT in full. The only exception to this arises where the right of action accrued before 31 March 1982, for here 1982 rebasing means the right of action is acquired at its 1982 value (see chapter 8). Normally, this equals the sums paid in damages or in settlement and so CGT is avoided.

A statutory relief applies to certain kinds of right of action (CGTA 1979 s.19(5)). Sums paid to an individual are exempt from CGT if they are damages or compensation for any wrong suffered in his person or in his profession or vocation. This relief, inter alia, includes damages for personal injury or defamation, and applies whether the damages are received by the individual or by his relatives or personal representatives.

Other rights of action are relieved in practice by extra statutory concession (ESC dated 19 December 1988). The main points are as follows:

(1) A right of action is treated as exempt if it arises out of a matter which is not an asset for CGT purposes.
(2) A right of action is relieved if it arises out of an asset, which is relieved from CGT. Examples given include private residences, retirement relief, and roll-over relief.
(3) Where neither of these two reliefs applies, damages or sums paid in compromise of the action may be treated as derived from the asset from which the action arose. This means they count as a part disposal of that asset, and accordingly an appropriate proportion of that asset's base value and indexation allowance may be deducted in computing the gain.

BES shares (CGTA 1979 s.149C)

The business expansion scheme was introduced in 1983-84 as a replacement for the business start-up scheme which operated for 1981-82 and 1982-83. Under the business expansion scheme relief from income tax is available for qualifying individuals who subscribe for new shares in qualifying companies. An individual may claim relief on up to £40,000 per year. To qualify for the relief both the company and the individual concerned must comply with certain conditions for five and three years respectively, and, in particular the shares must not be sold for five years. If the various conditions are not satisfied, the relief is withdrawn, giving rise to an income tax charge for the year relief was originally given. BES issues are now subject to an overriding maximum of £500,000 per company (FA 1988 s.51). Shares in companies constructing dwellings for letting on assured tenancies qualify for the relief, and here the maximum a company may raise is £5m (FA 1988 s.50).

Neither a chargeable gain nor an allowable loss can accrue on the disposal of BES shares if the following three conditions are satisfied:

(1) the shares were issued after 18 March 1986;

Exempt intangibles

(2) the shares were granted BES relief;
(3) the BES relief has not been withdrawn.

The exemption normally only applies on a disposal by the person to whom the shares were originally issued. But if that person disposes of the shares to his spouse, the spouse qualifies for the exemption as well. If some of the taxpayer's shares in a company are BES shares and some are not, any disposal is identified first with the BES shares (CGTA 1979 s.149C (4)).

If BES shares which qualify for the capital gains tax exemption are involved in a share-for-share exchange or in a reconstruction or amalgamation, the reliefs described in chapter 21 do not apply. This means the new shares are acquired for CGT purposes at their then market value, with the BES exemption relieving the gain on the original BES shares.

The exemption does not apply to BES shares issued before 18 March 1986. But any gain accruing on the disposal of such shares is calculated in the normal way, using the full cost of the shares and ignoring any income tax relief given. In this way relief is given on the expenditure for both capital gains tax and income tax purposes. If however a loss arises on disposal and income tax relief has been given and not withdrawn, the relevant allowable expenditure is reduced by the lower of the loss and the income tax relief given.

Personal equity plans (CGTA 1979 s.149D)

Personal equity plans were originally introduced in 1986, and what are now called old-style PEPs were governed by the Personal Equity Plan Regulations 1986. In 1989 the rules relating to PEPs were relaxed and PEPs are now governed by the Personal Equity Plan Regulations 1989.

In essence a PEP is a contractual arrangement between an individual investor and an approved financial intermediary known as the plan manager. The investor pays a subscription to the manager and the manger then invests this in plan investments which he holds as nominee for the investor. The basic rule is that plan investments must be quoted UK equities but half of the fund may be invested in unit trusts or investment trusts, and cash on deposit is allowed as well. An individual cannot transfer investments to a plan in specie save by renouncing shares allotted to him in a public issue.

Two tax reliefs are available to PEPs. First, dividends on plan investments are free of income tax, and second, any gains are

Personal equity plans (CGTA 1979 s.149D)

exempt from CGT. Under the 1986 Regulations, these reliefs only applied if the plan was or became a mature portfolio, but now plan investments are exempt from the outset. Subscriptions to PEPs do not attract relief, whether against income tax or CGT.

It is to be noted that PEP gains are exempt even if a sum representing the gain is withdrawn from the plan immediately afterwards. Relief is also given where plan investments are withdrawn in specie, for in those circumstances the gain accruing prior to the withdrawal is exempted by deeming the withdrawal to be a disposal at market value.

Originally, losses on plan investments were allowable against gains outside the plan. The position was altered from 18 January 1988 and now plan losses are not allowable against gains outside the plan. So long as they remain in the plan, shares are pooled separately from other shares of the same class belonging to the plan investor.

A taxpayer may only subscribe a limited amount to a PEP in any given year. Under the 1986 Regulations, the limit was applied by calendar year and for 1988 and 1989 it stood at £3,000. Under the 1989 Regulations, the limit is applied by years of assessment and stands at £4,800 for 1989-90. As will be apparent, the calendar year 1989 overlaps with the year of assessment 1989-90, and the taxpayer may make a subscription for both. Accordingly, a total of £7,800 may be subscribed in the period 1 January 1989 to 5 April 1990.

The annual limit is not shared between spouses, so each spouse may subscribe the maximum amount in any year. Over the years, the combination of annual subscriptions and tax-free capital gains and income enables substantial PEPs to be built up, particularly for married couples who both subscribe.

Chapter 15
Exempt Chattels

Chattles not exceeding £6,000 in value (CGTA 1979 s.128)

Any gain accruing on the disposal of an asset is not chargeable if the asset is tangible moveable property and the consideration does not exceed £6,000. Allowable losses are expressly excluded from this exemption, but, in computing any loss on the disposal of tangible moveable property, the consideration is deemed to be £6,000 if it is, in fact, less.

If the consideration exceeds £6,000, a form of marginal relief may apply to any gains. This relief requires £6,000 to be deducted from the actual consideration, and the resultant sum is then multiplied by five-thirds. If the gain exceeds the figure which ensues from that multiplication, the excess is exempt.

The limit of the chattel exemption is periodically increased. From 1982 to 1989 it stood at £3,000, and it was raised to the present level of £6,000 from 6 April 1989 (FA 1989 s.123).

Example
On 15 April 1989 Mr A sells a painting for £8,400 which he purchased for £500 in April 1982.

Increase in the retail prices index April 1982-April 1989: 0.410

Proceeds			£8,400
Less:cost			£ 500
			£7,900
Less: indexation allowance: 0.410 × £500			£ 205
			£7,695
Less: marginal relief			
gain		£7,695	
proceeds	£8,400		
less	£6,000		
	£2,400 × $\frac{5}{3}$ =	£4,000	
			£3,695

92

Foreign currency (CGTA 1979 s.133)

Chargeable gain £4,000

Wasting assets (CGTA 1979 s.127)

No chargeable gain or allowable loss can accrue on the disposal of a wasting asset which is tangible moveable property. Wasting assets are assets with a predictable life of less than 50 years (see p 8) but this exemption is less important than it appears. It does not apply to an asset if:

(1) the person making the disposal has used the asset solely for business purposes and has or could have claimed any capital allowance; or
(2) the person making the disposal has incurred any expenditure on the asset which has otherwise qualified in full for any capital allowance.

The effect of this exclusion is that the exemption of wasting assets does not apply to business property. The assets so excluded are the same as those which are excluded from the writing off of allowable expenditure (see p 34).

Vehicles (CGTA 1979 s.130)

A mechanically propelled road vehicle constructed or adapted for the carriage of passengers is not a chargeable asset unless it is of a type not commonly used as a private vehicle and unsuitable to be so used. One application of this exemption is to antique cars.

Medals and decorations (CGTA 1979 s.131)

A gain is not chargeable if it accrues on the disposal of a decoration awarded for valour or gallant conduct. This exemption however only operates if the person making the disposal acquired the decoration otherwise than for money or money's worth.

Foreign currency (CGTA 1979 s.133)

Gains accruing on the disposal of foreign currency are not chargeable in certain circumstances. The disposal must be by

Exempt chattels

an individual, and the currency must have been acquired by him for the personal expenditure outside the United Kingdom of himself or his family and dependants. The expenditure can include the maintenance of any residence abroad. There is a corresponding exemption for foreign currency bank accounts (see p 88).

Chapter 16

Retirement Relief

Introduction

A measure of relief has always been afforded to elderly taxpayers disposing of a business on retirement. The relief was originally conferred by CGTA 1979 s.124 and over the years it became increasingly supplemented by extra statutory concessions and statements of practice. The relief was recast in 1985 in what is perhaps the least intelligible part of the entire CGT code (FA 1985 ss.69 and 70 and Sch 20).

Retirement (FA 1985 s.69(1))

Retirement relief is available if the taxpayer has satisfied one of two conditions:

(a) he has attained 60; or
(b) he has retired through ill health and will remain permanently unable to return to his former work.

Retirement relief is applied automatically once the taxpayer is 60, but a claim is needed if the taxpayer has retired earlier through ill health, and medical evidence is required (FA 1985 Sch 20 para 3). Somewhat paradoxically, once the taxpayer has attained 60 retirement is not a precondition for the relief, and there is nothing to stop the taxpayer continuing to work or starting a new business.

Qualifying disposals (FA 1985 ss.69 and 70)

Retirement relief is available on the disposal of the following kinds of asset:

(a) unincorporated businesses;

Retirement relief

    (b) shares in family trading companies in which the taxpayer is a full-time working director;
    (c) assets used by a partnership of which the taxpayer is a member or by a family trading company of which he is a full-time working director;
    (d) certain business assessts held by trustees of interest in possession settlements;
    (e) assets held or provided by the taxpayer for the purposes of his employment.

Disposals of assets within (a) and (b) above are known as material disposals of business assessts. Disposals within (c),(d), and (e) are referred to as associated disposals, trustees' disposals and employee's disposals respectively. The generic term for all five kinds of disposal is qualifying disposal (FA 1985 Sch 20 para 4).

Qualifying period (FA 1985 Sch 20 paras 4(2), 14 and 16)

For a disposal to be a qualifying disposal, various conditions have to be satisfied during what is called the qualifying period. This normally ends with the date of disposal, but on certain kinds of disposal it ends earlier. For retirement relief to be available at all the qualifying period must be at least one year. For it to be available in full the period must be ten years.

    If the qualifying period is less than ten years, it can be extended if the taxpayer was previously concerned in the carrying on of another business. It can also be extended if the taxpayer acquired the business or shares from his spouse, but here, if the acquisition was inter vivos, the taxpayer cannot obtain more relief than the spouse would have done.

Amount available for relief (FA 1985 Sch.20 paras 13 and 15)

Retirement relief is not available on all gains accruing on qualifying disposals. It is only available on gains up to what is known as the amount available for relief. The basic rule is that the amount available for relief is £125,000 plus an amount equal to half the gains on qualifying disposals in excess of that limit, up to a maximum of £500,000.

    This basic rule only applies if the qualifying period has lasted at least ten years. If the qualifying period is less than ten years, the figures of £125,000 and £500,000 are pro rata reduced, falling to a minimum of £12,500 and £50,000 when the qualifying period is precisely one year.

The amount available for relief is available once only to each taxpayer. In other words, once a taxpayer's gains on qualifying disposals have exceeded £500,000, no subsequent disposal can attract relief. But if the £500,000 limit has not been exceeded, the shortfall may be carried forward to subsequent qualifying disposals.

On disposals before 6 April 1988, the amount available for relief was simply £125,000, pro rata reduced where the qualifying period was less than ten years. Taxpayers who had exhausted that limit now have the opportunity for further relief, on gains up to half the difference between £125,000 and £500,000, ie on gains up to £187,500.

Chargable business assets (FA 1985 Sch 20 para 12)

Retirement relief is only available insofar as the assets disposed of are chargeable business assets or, where company shares are disposed of, insofar as the company's chargeable assets are business assets. Chargeable business assets are assets which satisfy two conditions, namely:

(a) any gain accruing on the disposal of the asset would, apart from retirement relief, be chargeable; and
(b) the asset is used by the individual or company concerned for the purposes of a trade, profession, vocation, office or employment.

The main significance of this definition is that it excludes assets held as investments. By this rather circuitous route, retirement relief thus effectively excludes investment businesses.

Unincorporated businesses (FA 1985 s.69)

If the disposal of an unincorporated business is to be a qualifying disposal, the business must have been owned by the taxpayer throughout the qualifying period. However disincorporation is allowed for, in that the qualifying period can include any period during which the business was owned by a family trading company of which the taxpayer was a working director.

A business is not a single asset, but merely the aggregation of all the assets used therein, including goodwill. Accordingly the relief is applied to the aggregate of the gains accruing on the chargeable business assets, after deducting therefrom any losses accruing on the disposal of the business.

Retirement relief applies where part of a business is disposed of. This most obviously covers the disposal of a partnership interest. But it also embraces the sole trader who sells or gives away part of his business. In cases of this kind it is sometimes difficult to decide whether part of the business has been disposed of or whether the disposal has simply been assets of a continuing and unaltered business. Problems of this kind most often arise with farmers and the test is whether the part disposal sufficiently interferes with the whole complex of activities and assets which make up the business (*McGregor v Adcock* [1977] STC 206; *Atkinson v Dancer* [1988] STC 758). In practice a disposal of over half a farm is almost always regarded as the disposal of part of the farming business.

Frequently the taxpayer closes his business down and then disposes of the assets. Such disposals are not disposals of the business, but they are relieved in their own right (FA 1985 s.69(4)). They count as material disposals provided they occur within one year of the closure or such longer period as the Revenue allow. The qualifying period ends with the closure rather than the sale, and the closure is the date by which the taxpayer must have attained 60 or retired through ill health.

Shares in family trading companies (FA 1985 s.69)

A company counts as a trading company if its business is trading. It is a family company if one of two conditions are satisfied (FA 1985 Sch 20 para 1). Either 25 per cent or more of the voting rights must be exercisable by the taxpayer or 51 per cent or more of the voting rights must be exercisable by the taxpayer and his family, and 5 per cent by the taxpayer himself. Family includes spouses, siblings, ancestors and lineal descendants, and voting rights exercised by trustees are included if all actual or potential members of the trust are members of the taxpayer's family (FA 1985 Sch 20 para 1).

It is not sufficent that the company be the taxpayer's family company. He must also be a full-time working director. This means he must devote a substantial part of his time to either (a) that company or (b) that company and others in the same group or (c) that company and others in the same commercial association of companies. The latter term is an unusual one in the UK tax code and means simply companies under common

Associated disposals (FA 1985 s.70(5))

control whose business are effectively a single undertaking (FA 1985 Sch 20 para 1(2)).

For a disposal of shares to be a qualifying disposal these various conditions must have been satisfied during the qualifying period, which ends with the date of the disposal. But if the business has been incorporated, the qualifying period may include the unincorporated phase if the taxpayer owned the business then.

Prima facie all the gain on shares in a company is eligible for relief, but a complication is introduced if the company's chargeable assets are not all chargeable business assets. In these circumstances relief applies only to an apportioned part of the gain.

In practice, family companies often cease trading before they are sold or go into liquidation. Such an early cessation does not jeopardise any retirement relief due to the shareholders provided the disposals take place within a year of the cessation or such longer period as the Revenue allow. But as with prior closures of an unincorporated business, the qualifying period ends with cessation, and the taxpayer must have attained 60 or retired through ill health before then.

Another common situation is that of the director/shareholder who eases off before disposing of his shares. He retains his entitlement to retirement relief providing he devotes at least ten hours per week to the company's affairs. But here the qualifying period ends when his full-time directorship ends, although it is not necessary for him to have attained 60 until the disposal occurs.

Retirement relief applies to groups of companies as well as to single companies. A disposal of shares in the parent counts as a material disposal provided the group as a whole is a trading group. The chargeable business asset test is applied to the assets of all the companies in the group, shares in group members being ignored. For these purposes a group is a parent and its 51 per cent subsidiaries, and apportionments are made in applying the chargeable business assets test to companies which are not wholly owned (FA 1985 Sch 20, para 8).

Associated disposals (FA 1985 s.70(5))

A disposal counts as an associated disposal if three conditions are satisfied. First the taxpayer must be making a qualifying disposal of a partnership interest or shares in a family trading company. Second, the asset concerned must have been used by the partnership or company whose shares are being disposed of. Third, the disposal must be associated with the taxpayer's withdrawal from participation in the business of the company or partnership.

One quirk is that the asset disposed of must be a chargeable business asset (FA 1985 Sch 20 para 6). That means inter alia it cannot be an investment, and as a result a disposal cannot be an associated disposal if the partnership or company has paid a market rent. Partial relief is allowed if and to the extent that any rent has been below market levels (FA 1985 Sch 20 para 10). Apportionments are also made if the assest was used by the partnership or company for part only of the taxpayer's ownership.

Trustees' disposals (FA 1985 s.70(3))

Retirement relief can apply to a disposal by trustees if the trust is a fixed-interest trust. The life tenant is known as the qualifying beneficiary and retirement relief is available on a disposal of either (a) trust assets used by him in an unincorporated business or (b) trust shares in any company which is his family trading company and of which he is full-time working director. But these reliefs are only available if the disposal takes place within a year or such longer period as the Revenue allow, of the cessation of the business or, as the case may be, the qualifying beneficiary's retirement as a director. He must also have attained 60 or retired through ill health before such retirement or cessation.

Employee's disposals (FA 1985 s.70(1))

Although retirement relief primarily affects the self-employed and family companies, employees are entitled to it in respect of assets provided or held for the purposes of their employment. The disposal may occur either when the employee retires or within a year or such longer period as the Revenue allow thereafter. The employee must have attained 60 or retired through ill health and the qualifying period ends with the disposal.

Chapter 17

Death

Deemed reacquisition (CGTA 1979 s.49(1))

When an individual dies all his assets are deemed to be acquired at market value by his personal representatives. But they are not treated as disposed of by the deceased, and as a result, death is the occasion of a new tax-free base value for all the deceased's assets.

Allowable losses (CGTA 1979 s.49(2))

Allowable losses accruing to the deceased in the year of his death may be relieved against the deceased's chargeable gains of that and the preceding three years. This is an exception to the general rule that losses cannot be carried back (see p 5). The deceased's losses cannot be carried forward and set against gains subsequently realised by the personal representatives.

Personal representatives (CGTA 1979 s.49(3))

The term personal representatives includes executors, administrators and persons performing an equivalent function under foreign systems of law (CGTA 1979 s.155). Personal representatives are treated as a single continuing body of persons who have the residence and domicile of the deceased.

Once residue is ascertained, the personal representatives cease to be personal representatives in relation to any assets they retain (cf *Stamp Duties Comr v Livingstone* [1964] 3 All ER 692 and *IRC v Matthew's Executors* [1984] STC 386). If the retained assets are settled by the will, the personal representatives become trustees and the assets are settled property. If the assets are not settled, the personal representatives hold them as nominees for those entitled.

Death

Gains and losses accruing to personal representatives during administration are chargeable or allowable in the normal way. Personal representatives are entitled to the same basic annual exemption as individuals for the year in which the deceased dies and for the two subsequent years (CGTA 1979 Sch 1 para 4). Currently this exemption stands at £5,000 (see p 59).

In computing any gains or losses, personal representatives may deduct valuation and other costs incurred in obtaining probate, for such expenditure is incurred in establishing title (*IRC v Richards Executors* [1971] 1 WLR 571). On estates under £400,000 the Revenue allow either the actual costs or a notional figure determined by a published scale (see SP 7/81).

Legatees (CGTA 1979 ss. 47 and 49 (4))

Disposals by personal representatives to legatees are ignored for CGT purposes. Accordingly the legatee is treated as acquiring the asset on the deceased's death at its probate value. The term 'legatee' does not simply mean specific or pecuniary legatees: for CGT purposes the term extends to anybody who takes under a will or intestacy. It also includes trustees where the deceased's will has constituted a trust.

Deeds of variation (CGTA 1979 s.49)

So long as all the beneficiaries under a will or intestacy are sui juris and over 18, they may, as a matter of general law vary the destination of the deceased's estate. Such a variation is not a disposal for CGT purposes if the following conditions are satisfied:

(1) the variation is effected in writing;
(2) it is made within two years of the deceased's death;
(3) an election is made to the inspector within six months of the variation;
(4) none of the parties to the variation receive any extraneous consideration.

A variation which satisfies these conditions may be made either before or after the assets to which it relates have been distributed. In practice, the main advantage of the relief is to avoid the tiresome valuations and calculations which would otherwise obtain when the strict entitlements under a will are varied. The relief corresponds to the relief for inheritance tax conferred by IHTA

Deeds of variation (CGTA 1979 s.49)

1984 s.142. The 1989 Budget included proposals to restrict the IHT relief, but these did not apply to CGT and were in any event withdrawn.

V Deferrals

Chapter 18

Hold-over Relief

Introduction

Gifts and other non arm's-length disposals are treated as taking place at market value (see chapter 4). As a result, a gain can accrue to the donor even though he has received nothing for the asset. That in turn means he has to find money to pay the tax even though the disposal which occasions the charge has not itself generated funds.

In the early years of CGT this injustice was unremedied. In 1978, however, a form of hold-over relief was introduced for gifts of business assets, and that relief passed into the 1979 consolidation as CGTA 1979 s.126. In 1980, general hold-over relief for all gifts to individuals and trustees was introduced by FA 1980 s.79 and this was extended to deemed disposals of settled property in 1982. Section 126 remained on the statute book, but was restricted to gifts of business assets to companies.

The general relief for gifts, together with other reliefs such as that on death (see chapter 17) meant that CGT was essentially a charge on realised gains, payable only in respect of transactions which generated funds to pay the tax. Unfortunately, the Government saw fit in 1989 to disturb this satisfactory state of affairs. Because hold-over relief played a minor part in facilitating certain forms of avoidance, it was restricted with effect from 14 March 1989 (FA 1989 s.124). General hold-over relief in s.79 has been repealed, and instead s.126 has been been restored and expanded to continue hold-over relief for gifts and other non-arm's length disposals of business assets. In addition, a new s.147A allows relief on certain disposals involving trusts heritage property and political parties.

Gifts of business assets (CGTA 1979 ss.126, 126A and 126B and Sch 4)

Two categories of business asset are eligible for hold-over relief under s.126, namely assets used for business purposes and certain shareholdings. Assets qualify if they are used in a business carried on either by the donor himself or by his family company. Shares attract the relief if the company is either a trading company or the holding company of a trading group. If the company is unquoted, the relief is available no matter how small the donor's holding is, but where the company is quoted, the company must be the donor's family company.

The term family company has the same meaning as for retirement relief purposes (see chapter 16). A company is the donor's family company if he owns 25 per cent or more of the voting rights himself, or if he owns 5 per cent and he and his family 51 per cent. It will be noted that under these requirements, the same company can be a family company in relation to many different individuals. There is no requirement that the donor be a full-time working director, or even a director at all.

Only a proportion of the gain accruing on assets is eligible for relief if the asset was not used for business purposes throughout the donor's ownership. So too, apportioned relief is available where the asset is a building, part of which is used for business purposes and part not.

An apportionment may also be required with shares. This becomes necessary in the same circumstances as with retirement relief, namely where the company's chargeable assets include non-business assets. In this situation the gain eligible for relief is reduced by a fraction, of which the numerator is the value of the assets used for business purposes and the denominator is the value of the company's total chargeable assets. Where the company is the holding company of a group, the chargeable assets of the group as a whole are looked at, shares in the subsidiaries being ignored.

For relief under s.126 to be available the recipient must be resident in the UK. The recipient may be another individual, a trust, or a company. Where the recipient is a company, it is not sufficient for the company alone to be resident in the UK. The relief is precluded if the company in controlled by non-residents and those non-residents are connected with the donor.

Settled business assets (CGTA 1979 Sch 4 para 2)

As well as being available on gifts by individuals, relief under s.126 may also be claimed when a person becomes absolutely entitled to settled property. The assets and shares which attract the relief are broadly the same as with individuals. Assets qualify if they are used in a business carried on by the trustees or, if the trust is a fixed-interest trust, by the life tenant. Shares qualify if the company is unquoted or if the trustees control 25 per cent or more of the voting rights. Any claim for the relief must be made both by the trustees and the person becoming absolutely entitled, although if it is another set of trustees who are becoming absolutely entitled, it is the disponor trustees alone who need claim.

Agricultural property (CGTA 1979 Sch 4 paras 1 and 3)

One category of asset attracts relief under s.126 even if it is not used in the donor's business or that of his family company. This is farmland qualifying for agriculture property relief under inheritance tax (IHTA 1984 s.116). This extension of relief applies both to gifts by individuals and to deemed disposals of settled property, and it is available regardless of whether the disposal is in fact a transfer of value for inheritance tax purposes.

Relief under s.147A (CGTA 1979 ss.147A and 147B)

Relief under s.147A is available on certain gifts by individuals if the recipient is either another individual or a settlement. Relief can also apply on certain occasions on which a person becomes absolutely entitled to settled property, although here too the person becoming absolutely entitled must be either an individual or another trust. Section 147A relief never applies if the recipient is a company and, as with s.126, the recipient must be resident in the UK.

The main category of gift to which s.147A applies is gifts by individuals which are immediately chargeable transfers for inheritance tax purposes and not potentially exempt. Under inheritance tax, all lifetime transfers by individuals are potentially exempt unless the recipient is a company or a discretionary trust (IHTA 1984 s.3A). Since gifts to companies are not within s.147A at all, it is, therefore, only gifts to discretionary trusts which attract s.147A relief.

For a gift to be within s.147A, it is not necessary for IHT to be paid. Accordingly, the relief applies even if the gift is free of IHT because it falls within the donor's nil rate band. The same applies if it is covered by his IHT basic annual exemption.

Section 147A definitely applies in one situation where a person becomes absolutely entitled to settled property, namely where an interest vests under an accumulation and maintenance trust (IHTA 1984 s.71(4)). It is a question of some difficulty as to whether s.147A relief is available when an individual or another trust becomes absolutely entitled as against a discretionary trust.

Hold-over relief

Such an event does not attract potential exemption for IHT purposes. Some such events can be treated for the purposes of IHTA 1984 as chargeable transfers, but not all are so treated, for the occasion of one discretionary trust becoming absolutely entitled as against another is ignored for IHT purposes (see IHTA 1984 ss.2(3) and 65). For this reason, the better view is that in law s.147A relief does not apply to deemed disposals out of discretionary trusts.

The other disposals to which s.147A applies are defined by reference to the IHT reliefs for transfers involving political parties, heritage property and maintenance funds for historic buildings. Some of these transfers may be made by individuals, and otherwise they are notional transfers affecting settled property.

Operation of the reliefs (CGTA 1979 s.126(3)-(6) and (9)-(10) and s.147A(3)-(9))

Both the relief under s.126 and that under s.147A are dependent on a claim. Where the recipient is a trust, the claim is made by the donor alone. Otherwise, the claim has to be a joint claim by the donor and the recipient.

The relief operates on the gain which would otherwise accrue apart from the claim. This is the gain after deducting the indexation allowance. This gain is deducted from the donor's proceeds of disposal, so as to prevent a chargeable gain from accruing to him. It is also deducted from the donee's acquisition cost, and this reduced figure constitutes his acquisition cost both generally and for the purposes of computing the indexation allowance.

Example

Mr Smith is an accountant in sole practice. He acquired freehold office premises in 1978 for £50,000. On 31 March 1982 the office was worth £100,000. On 30 April 1989, when the property was worth £200,000, he gave it to his son James who sells it on 31 May 1992 for £250,000.

Mr Smith and James make a hold-over election in relation to the 1989 gift.

1989-90: Disposal by Mr Smith

	Proceeds (MV)	£200,000
Less:	Acquisition cost (1982 MV)	£100,000
	Unindexed gain	£100,000
Less:	Indexation allowance	£ 43,900
	Held-over gain	£ 56,100

	1992-3: Disposal by James		
	Proceeds of disposal		£250,000
Less:	Acquisition cost		
	1989 MV	£200,000	
	Held-over gain	£ 56,100	
		£143,900	£143,900
	Unindexed gain		£106,100
Less:	Indexation allowance		
	0.11 (est) × £143,900		£ 15,829
	Chargeable gain		£ 20,271

As well as being available on gifts where no consideration passes, the reliefs also apply on non arm's-length disposals where some consideration passes, but not the full value of the asset. Here, the relief is available in full if the actual consideration is less than the donor's base cost. But if the consideration exceeds the base cost, the gain able to be held over is reduced by the excess. For these purposes, the comparison is between base cost plus indexation and consideration, rather than between base cost and consideration. Accordingly, in a case where the actual consideration equals the indexed base cost, hold-over relief is lost to the extent of the indexation allowance.

A hold-over disposal can be the occasion on which IHT is immediately payable, or becomes so because the donor fails to survive seven years. Where this happens, any IHT attributable to the asset is allowed as a deduction in computing the donee's gain if and when he disposes of the asset. The deduction cannot exceed what would otherwise be his indexed gain.

The claw-back (FA 1981 s.79; CGTA 1979 s.126C)

A held-over gain becomes chargeable if the recipient ceases to be resident in the UK without having first disposed of the asset on which the held-over gain accrued. This claw-back applies whether the gain was held over under the old general relief or under the present CGTA 1979 ss.126 and 147A. If the recipient is an individual, the claw-back only occurs if he ceases to be a UK resident within six years of the end of the year of assessment in which the hold-over relief disposal took place. But where the recipient is a settlement, the claw-back may be effected if the settlement becomes non-resident at any time.

The claw-back is avoided for individual recipients if the recipient becomes non-resident because he is employed in a job whose duties are performed wholly abroad. But this avoidance

Hold-over relief

whose duties are performed wholly abroad. But this avoidance of the claw-back is only provisional, for the claw-back still occurs if the period of non-residence exceeds three years or the recipient disposes of the asset.

In the first instance, any gain clawed back is assessed on the recipient. Tax under this assessment is payable in the normal way on 6 December next following the year of assessment concerned. If it is not so paid during the twelve months following that date, then it may be assessed on the donor of the hold-over disposal. But such an assessment may not be made once six years have elapsed from the year of assessment of that disposal.

The possibility of a held-over gain being assessed on the donor is a real one, for once a recipient is non-resident, the Revenue will have difficulty in recovering tax from him. In practice, donors should not concur in a hold-over relief election without taking appropriate security from the recipient.

The claw-back does not apply if the recipient is a company, for company migration is in any event the occasion of a deemed disposal (see p 135). But a modified form of claw-back occurs if the company is controlled by a trust connected with the donor and the trust migrates. In these circumstances the trustees may be assessed on the held-over gain if the company has not disposed of the asset and, if the trustees do not pay the tax, the donor may be assessed up to six years after the year of assessment of the gift.

Payment of tax by instalments (CGTA 1979 s.7A)

The withdrawal of general hold-over relief means that CGT may be payable on transactions which do not themselves generate the requisite cash. Limited relief for this unsatisfactory state of affairs is offered by the right to pay the tax by instalments.

For the instalment option to be available two conditions must be satisfied. First, the disposal must not be one of those on which hold-over relief could be claimed under CGTA 1979 ss.126 and 147A. Second the gifted asset must be either land, unquoted shares, or shares out of what was previously a controlling shareholding.

If these conditions are satisfied the tax may be paid by ten annual instalments. The instalments are not interest-free. All outstanding instalments become payable if the gifted asset is sold, unless the gift was made by an individual and he and the donee are unconnected.

Chapter 19

Replacement of Business Assets

Roll-over relief (CGTA 1979 ss.115–21)

A relief, known as roll-over relief, applies where a trader replaces certain kinds of business asset. Any indexed gain accruing on what are termed 'the old assets' may be carried forward and deducted from the acquisition cost of the new assets. But although this basic concept is simple, the legislation enacting it is badly drafted and contains a minefield of traps for the unwary. In many cases, the rigour of the law has been tempered by concession, and indeed, the practical importance of the relief makes it surprising that it has not been comprehensively recast.

Persons eligible (CGTA1979 ss.115 and 121)

Although the legislation and this chapter are expressed in terms of trade and persons carrying on a trade, the relief is extended inter alia to professions, vocations, offices, and employments. As a result it is clear that the relief applies to virtually all non-investment businesses. The commercial letting of furnished holiday accommodation is deemed to be a trade for these purposes (FA1984 s.50 and Sch 11).

At one time the old and new assets had to be used by the taxpayer in the same trade. Now this is no longer so, and indeed it is accepted that the trades can be successive rather than simultaneous. Thus a solicitor who retires from practice and starts a shop can roll the proceeds of his former office into the acquisition of the new shop.

What is essential is that one and the same taxpayer carries on the trade, sells the old assets, and acquires the new ones. Thus the relief does not apply if the old assets are sold by a husband and the new ones are bought by his wife, or if the assets are owned by a trust and the trade is carried on by a beneficiary. Exceptions to this rule are made where the trade is carried on by the taxpayer's family company and where groups of companies are involved.

The classes of asset (CGTA1979 s.118)

Not all assets used in business are eligible for roll-over relief. The legislation defines a number of classes of asset which attract the relief and both the old and the new assets must fall within one of these classes. Originally they had to be in the same class but this ceased to be so many years ago.

The classes of asset are as follows:

1(A)(1)	Any building or part of a building and any permanent or semi-permanent structure
1(A)(2)	Land
1(B)	Fixed plant and machinery
2	Ships, aircraft and hovercraft
2A	Satellites, space stations and spacecraft (including launch vehicles)
3	Goodwill
4	Milk and potato quotas

Buildings and land only come within these classes if they are both used and occupied for the purposes of the trade. The use and occupation must be real: thus land does not qualify if the trader intends to use it for business purposes but sells it before he does so (*Temperley v Visibell Ltd* [1974] STC 64). Where part only of a building is used for business purposes, appropriate apportionments are made to apply the relief to that part (*Todd v Mudd* [1987] STC 141).

The third class, fixed plant and machinery is difficult to identify. It does not mean plant and machinery which is a fixed asset in accountancy terms, but simply plant and machinery which does not move. Vehicles and earth-moving equipment are thus excluded, and in general the term comprehends immobile equipment which has not become a fixture (*Williams v Evans* [1982] STC 498).

Classes 2A and 4 were added in 1988 (FA1988 s.112). But the additions are retrospective in that they took effect from 28 July 1987 and 30 October 1987 respectively. Roll-over relief applies to these classes if the old assets were disposed of, or the new assets acquired, after these dates (see IR Press Release, 11 July 1988).

Old assets — general (CGTA1979 s.115)

To be eligible for relief the old assets, whatever class they are in, must have been used for the purposes of the taxpayer's trade throughout his ownership. But for assets owned on 31 March 1982 this rule is relaxed. It is only necessary that such assets have been used in the taxpayer's trade since the new base date (FA 1988 Sch 8 para 9).

An apportionment is allowed where business use has only subsisted for part of the taxpayer's period of ownership. The apportionment is achieved by deeming the asset to be two separate assets, one representing the business phase of use and the other the non-business phase (s.115(6)).

New assets (CGTA1979 s.115)

The statutory requirement is that an asset only counts as a new asset if on acquisition it is taken into use for business purposes. This requirement used to prove more troublesome than most, for it excluded relief in many situations where it ought to have applied, notably where a partner increased his share in partnership assets or where a tenant-farmer bought the freehold. To some extent the difficulties of this requirement have now been overcome, but only by concessions (Extra Statutory Concessions D22-D25).

The gist of the relevant concessions is as follows:

(1) Enhancement expenditure on existing assets is treated as expenditure on new assets if the assets are already business assets or if they are taken into use when the works are completed.
(2) Assets count as new assets even if they have to be improved before being taken into use.
(3) The acquisition of an interest in an asset which is already in use is treated as the acquisition of a new asset.
(4) The division of assets in specie on the dissolution of a partnership is treated as the acquisition of a new asset.

Once the taxpayer has acquired the new assets and taken them into use, the relief is not jeopardised if he ceases to use them thereafter. The only restriction to watch is that relief is not available unless the new assets are genuinely acquired for business use. An intention, at the time of acquisition, to realise a gain on their subsequent disposal fatal.

Replacement of business assets
Time limits (CGTA1979 s.115)

The new assets have to be acquired during a period which begins 12 months before the disposal of the old assets and ends three years thereafter. It is thought that the normal CGT rules apply to determine the dates of disposal and acquisition (cf p 11 ante). The Revenue have discretion to extend the time limits, but in practice they will only do so if the taxpayer can provide a good reason why he has not been able to acquire the new asset within the statutory period.

Roll-over relief is not available unless the taxpayer claims it. There is no special time limit, so the normal rule applies — ie the claim must be made within six years of the chargeable period to which it relates.

Operation of the relief

A gain is only wholly rolled over if the consideration received for the old asset is invested in full in the new assets. It is to be stressed that it is not sufficient if only an amount equal to the gain is so invested. If the proceeds of the old asset are fully reinvested, the gain otherwise chargeable on the old asset is not chargeable and instead, it is deducted from the acquisition cost of the new. The gain thus rolled over is the gain arrived at after the indexation allowance has been made and any indexation allowance on the new asset is based on its acquisition cost as reduced by roll-over relief.

Strictly the legislation requires the self-same consideration received for the old assets to be invested in the new assets. But this strict construction is plainly wrong, for the legislation contemplates new assets being acquired up to twelve months before the disposal of the old. Accordingly all that is required in practice is the reinvestment of an amount equivalent to the proceeds of the old assets.

Example
ABC Ltd is a trading company which purchased a freehold shop in July 1983 for £25,000. In August 1985 it sells the shop for £40,000 and in December 1985 it purchased a replacement for £45,000. This shop is sold in March 1988 for £65,000 and there is no replacement.

  Indexed rises are as follows
  RI   July 1983/RD August 1985 = 0.131
  RI   December 1985/RD March 1988 = 0.084

New depreciating assets (CGTA1979 s.117)

August 1985:
  Proceeds   £40,000
  Less: Cost   £25,000
  Gross gain   £15,000
  Less: Indexation allowance
  July 1983 – August 1985   £ 3,275
  Gain (rolled over)   £11,725
  Base cost of new shop £45,000 – £11,275   £33,275
March 1988
  Proceeds   £65,000
  Less: Cost   £33,275
  Gross gain   £31,725
  Less: Indexation allowance
  December 1985 – March 1988
  $0.084 \times £33,275$ £ 2,795
Chargeable gain   £28,930

Partial reinvestment (CGTA1979 s.116)

All may not be lost if part only of the proceeds of the old assets is invested in new assets. The part not reinvested can be deducted from the gain, and, if it is less than the gain, the amount by which it is less is eligible for roll-over relief.

New depreciating assets (CGTA 1979 s.117)

A depreciating asset is an asset which is either a wasting asset or will become one within ten years. Wasting assets are assets with a predictable life of less than 50 years and include plant and machinery and short leases (see p 8). In the absence of special provision, there would be obvious avoidance possibilities in acquiring depreciating assets as new assets, for the tax on the rolled-over gain would be avoided when the life of the asset ended.

    These possibilities are countered by special rules which effectively prevent depreciating assets from counting as new assets. If the new asset is such an asset, the gain on the old asset is not rolled into it, but is held in suspense. It becomes chargeable after ten years or, if earlier, when the depreciating asset is sold or goes out of use. But if in the meantime the taxpayer has acquired a non-depreciating asset, then the whole suspended gain may be rolled into this third asset.

Replacement of business assets

1982 rebasing (FA 1988 Sch 9)

A special relief applies where an asset is disposed of on or after 6 April 1988 and that asset was the new asset on a prior roll-over relief claim. It applies if the old asset in the claim was acquired before 31 March 1982 and disposed of between then and 5 April 1988. In these circumstances, the rolled-over gain deducted from the acquisition cost of the new asset is reduced by half. A similar relief can apply when the held-over gain on a new depreciating asset becomes chargeable. These reliefs are described above (see p 45-8).

Family companies (CGTA1979 s.120)

A taxpayer may claim roll-over relief if the use of the old and new assets is not by him but by his 'family company'. The term 'family company' bears the same meaning as for retirement relief purposes (see p 98). It is a company in which either the taxpayer alone has 25 per cent or more of the voting rights or he and his family have 51 per cent or more of the voting rights and he has at least 5 per cent. This relaxation of the relief does not apply unless both the disposal and the acquisition are by the taxpayer personally, and the better view is that the same company must use both the old and the new assets.

Groups (TA1970 s.276)

The CGT legislation provides that all trades carried on by member companies of a group are to be treated as a single trade for roll-over relief purposes. Of itself, this does not effect a great extension to the relief, for it merely means that the group member using an asset in a trade does not have to be the same as the group member disposing of it or acquiring it.

In practice, the availability of roll-over relief to groups is much extended by concession. The Revenue allow relief where one group member makes the disposal and another the aquisition (SP 8/81 and D19). A further concession is that property-holding group members are treated as trading where they hold assets used for trading purposes by other group members.

Group trades are not treated as a single trade where the disposal or acquisition is between group members (TA 1970 s.276(1)). This means an intra-group acquisition can count as an acquisition for roll-over relief purposes, albeit at the deemed no

Groups (TA1970 s.276)

loss-no gain consideration. Accordingly there is no reason in principle why the gain on an outside sale should not be rolled over into an intra-group acquisition, although if artificiality is involved, *Ramsay* principles may need to be considered.

If prior to a disposal outside the group, an asset is transferred from one group member to another, it is the use by the final group member which determines whether roll-over relief is available. This can work in favour of the taxpayer or the Revenue, depending on the uses by the companies concerned. If the final company is trading, use in any member's trade preserves roll-over relief. If the asset is not used at all while in the final company's ownership, roll-over relief is lost.

Chapter 20

Other Roll-over Reliefs

Transfer of business to a company (CGTA 1979 s.123)

A form of roll-over relief is available when an unincorporated business is transferred to a company. For this relief to apply in full the following conditions must be satisfied:

(1) the person transferring the business must be an individual or a partnership;
(2) the business must be transferred as a going concern;
(3) all the assets of the business apart from cash must be transferred to the company;
(4) the company must issue shares to the proprietor(s) of the business as the sole consideration for the transfer.

As will be apparent, a transaction which satisfies these conditions is effectively an exchange, for the proprietors of the business exchange the business for shares in the company. The business assets, therefore, are disposed of at market value, and the acquisition cost of the shares is the aggregate net value of the business transferred.

The relief requires the total gains on the business assets to be aggregated, and that aggregate is then reduced by any losses on the business assets. This aggregate net gain is then exempted from tax on the transfer, and an amount equal to the net gain is deducted from the acquisition cost of the shares. Accordingly, the gain is carried forward to the shares.

It is to be noted that it is the shares which are reduced by the net gain, and not the assets transferred to the company. The company acquires the assets at market value, and accordingly the relief operates as a rebasing of those assets. The company, if it so chooses, can sell the assets shortly thereafter free of CGT.

In one limited circumstance partial relief is available. This happens where the share issue is not the sole consideration for the transfer, and here a proportion of the gain is relieved, the proportion corresponding to the proportion of the total consideration the shares represent. In practice the Revenue do not treat the assumption of the business's liabilities by the company as consideration, and so if the consideration consists just of shares and the assumption of liabilities, relief is available in full (ESC 20 October 1988).

There is, however, a trap. The liabilities of the business may significantly reduce its value, so much so that the net worth of the business is less than the aggregate net gains on the business assets. This means the shares are worth less than the net gains, and in these circumstances, the acquisition cost of the shares is nil and the balance of the net gains is chargeable.

The relief is not subject to a claim and so applies automatically. Structuring the incorporation of a business to take advantage of the relief carries the following drawbacks:

(1) Ad valorem Stamp Duty is chargeable.
(2) Strictly, the trading stock of the unincorporated business is transferred to the company at market value.
(3) Assets cannot be kept out of the company.
(4) Shares cannot be spread around the family until after the transfer is concluded and the value of the business is reflected in the shares.

Compulsory purchase (CGTA 1979 s.111A)

A form of roll-over relief is available on compulsory acquisitions of land. Three conditions must be satisfied before this relief is available:

(1) The land must be disposed of to an authority with compulsory powers. The disposal need not result from the exercise of compulsory powers, provided such powers have been, or could be, obtained.
(2) The owner must not have advertised his land, or otherwise evinced an intention to dispose of it.
(3) The proceeds of the disposal must be used to purchase new land or an interest therein which does not qualify for the private residence exemption.

If these conditions are satisfied, the taxpayer can claim a form of roll-over relief, analogous to that for business assets (chapter 19). The consideration for the disposal is reduced to such a figure that secures that neither a gain nor a loss is realised, and a like reduction is made in the acquisition cost of the new land. For the relief to apply an unconditional contract for the acquisition

Other roll-over reliefs

of the new land must be entered into not earlier than one year before the compulsory disposal, and not later than three years thereafter.

Where only part of the consideration for the compulsory disposal is invested in the new land, the position is again the same as for business assets. Roll-over relief only applies if the part of the consideration not reinvested is less than the gain, and it is restricted to whatever of the gain is left after the amount not reinvested has been deducted.

If the new land is a lease with less than 60 years to run, the business assets rules as to depreciating assets apply (see p 117). This means the compulsory disposal will not qualify for roll-over relief as such, but the gain can be held over until the lease is sold, or until ten years have elapsed, whichever is sooner.

As noted above the new land must not be a residence which qualifies for the private residence relief. It is not enough that it does not qualify when it is bought, but it must not qualify at any time within the next six years. If at the outset it does not attract the private residence relief, but does so within the six-year period, any roll-over relief is withdrawn, and such assessments are made as are necessary.

Lost and destroyed assets (CGTA 1979 s.21)

Where an asset has been lost or destroyed the receipt of insurance monies or other compensation constitutes a disposal (CGTA 1979 s.20; see p 14). But a form of roll-over relief applies if the money is used to acquire a replacement asset. The relief must be claimed and the replacement must be acquired within one year of the money being received or such longer period as the Inspector may allow.

The effect of the relief is as follows:

(1) the consideration for the notional disposal of the old asset is treated as being of such an amount as will secure that neither a gain nor loss accrues; and
(2) a corresponding reduction is made in the consideration treated as given for the acquisition of the new asset. The reduction is equal to the difference between (i) the no gain/ no loss consideration for the old asset and (ii) the aggregate of the scrap value of that asset plus the insurance monies or other compensation received.

1982 rebasing (FA 1988 Sch 9)

If the asset is not lost or destroyed but is damaged, the receipt of any insurance monies or other compensation is not treated as a disposal if the money is:

(1) wholly applied in restoring the asset; or
(2) applied in restoring the asset, except for an amount which is not reasonably required for the purpose, and is small as compared with the money received as a whole;
(3) is small in amount as compared with the value of the asset.

In all these cases the sums which would, had there been a disposal, have been treated as consideration in the computation of a gain are deducted from the allowable expenditure otherwise attributable to the asset. They are thus brought into account as and when the asset is eventually disposed of.

1982 rebasing (FA 1988 Sch 9)

A further relief may apply if a disposal to which one of the reliefs described in this chapter applied took place between 31 March 1982 and 5 April 1988. If certain conditions are satisfied, the rolled-over gain deducted from the acquisition cost of the new asset is reduced by half. This relief is described above (see p 45–6).

Chapter 21

Reorganisations, Mergers and Reconstructions

Introduction

In certain transactions involving companies and their shareholders, shares or securities are replaced by other shares or securities. Technically these transactions involve a disposal of the old shares or securities and an acquisition of the new ones, but in substance the underlying investment remains the same.

In most cases the CGT legislation recognises the substance of these transactions, and treats the new shares or securities as the same asset as the old ones. The following four situations are thus protected:

(1) reorganisations and reductions of share capital;
(2) the conversion of securities;
(3) share for share exchanges within CGTA 1979 s.85;
(4) reconstructions and amalgamations.

The relief (CGTA 1979 ss.78-81)

A taxpayer's shares or securities before one of the transactions listed above are referred to as the original shares, and the shares or debentures he acquires thereafter are called the new holding. The basic rule is that the transaction occasions neither a disposal of the original shares nor an acquisition of the new holding. Instead the new holding is treated as the same asset as the original shares, acquired at the same time and for the same price. This means, inter alia, that 1982 rebasing and indexation on the subsequent disposal of the new holding are based on the time and cost of the acquistion of the original shares.

If as part of the transaction the shareholder gives any consideration, that consideration counts as consideration given for the old holding. But this provision does not apply if the new consideration exceeds the amount by which the value of the new holding exceeds the value of the original shares. For indexation purposes, the new consideration is treated as given at the time of the reorganisation (FA 1982 Sch 13 para 5).

The reverse situation is where the transaction involves a payment to the shareholder. Here such a payment is treated as the disposal of an interest in the original shares. In other words it constitutes a part disposal of the composite asset represented by the original shares and the new holding.

The reliefs do not apply where either the original shares or the new holding are qualifying corporate bonds (FA 1984 s.64 and Sch 13). Qualifying corporate bonds are exempt from CGT (see p 86). If they constitute the original shares, the new holding is treated as acquired at market value at the time of the relevant transaction. Where they constitute the new holding, the original shares are disposed of at market value, but any gain accruing is held over until the qualifying corporate bonds are disposed of. If the original shares were acquired before 1 April 1982 and disposed of before 6 April 1988, the postponed gain may in certain circumstances be halved (see p 45–8).

Reorganisations (CGTA 1979 ss.77-81)

A reorganisation is defined for the CGT purposes as any reorganisation or reduction of a company's share capital. The term reorganisation is itself further defined as including the following:

(a) any case where persons are, whether for payment or not, allotted shares in or debentures of the company in respect of and in proportion to their pre-existing holding in the company;

(b) any case where the company has more than one class of share and the rights attaching to any class are altered.

Since this definition of reorganisation is not exhaustive, a reorganisation within the general meaning of the term counts as a reorganisation even if not specifically mentioned. Unfortunately reorganisation has no precise meaning in company law. But one transaction not specifically mentioned which is a reorganisation is the division of shares in a company with only one class of shares into shares of different classes (*Dunstan v Young Austen and Young Ltd* [1987] STC 709, 720). An increase of capital is a reorganisation provided the new shares are acquired by existing shareholders because they are existing shareholders and in proportion to their existing beneficial holdings (*Drummond v Young Austen and Young Ltd* [1989] STC 69, CA).

Conversion of securities (CGTA 1979 ss.82-3)

The term 'conversion of securities' is defined as including the following:

(a) conversion of securities in a company into shares in a company;
(b) conversion of securities at the option of the holder as an alternative to redemption for cash;
(c) any exchange of securities required by Act of Parliament.

The term 'security' is defined in CGTA 1979 s.82(3)(b). A security can be secured or unsecured and the term includes any loan stock or similar security of any of the following:

(a) the UK or any foreign government;
(b) any public or local authority in the UK or elsewhere;
(c) any company.

As described above, a taxpayer who receives payment on the conversion of securities makes a part disposal of the composite asset represented by the old and new securities. But if the payment is small, it is not treated as a part disposal, but instead is deducted from the acquisition cost (see p 31).

Share-for-share exchanges (CGTA 1979 s.85)

The transactions so far described in this chapter have been internal in the sense that they involve only a single company. Share for share exchanges, by contrast involve two companies, namely the acquiring company, Company A, and the target company, Company B. The essence of the transaction is that shareholders in company B sell their shares to company A not for cash, but in consideration of company A issuing them with shares or debentures.

Only certain exchanges qualify for the relief outlined in this chapter. In particular, company A must satisfy one of the two conditions. Either it must have made a general offer to the shareholders in Company B or, after the exchange, it must hold at least a quarter of Company B's share capital.

It is not necessary for Company A to dilute its equity, for the relief applies as much where debentures are issued as where the issue is of shares. The term 'debenture' comprehends any document which creates or acknowledges a debt, and so includes loan stock, loan notes and other securities.

Many exchanges involve an earn-out element. In other words, Company A acquires the shares in Company B in consideration of (a) an immediate issue of shares or debentures and (b) a further issue of shares and debentures if certain profit targets are met. Strictly, the further issue cannot qualify for relief, for the asset acquired on the exchange is not shares or debentures but the contingent right to the future issue (*Marren v Ingles* [1980] STC 500; see p 25). But concessionary treatment is available if the contingent right can only be satisfied by an issue of shares or debentures (IR Press Release 26 April 1988). If the taxpayer so claims, the Revenue will treat the contingent right as a security and the satisfaction of it as a conversion of securities.

Reconstructions and amalgamations (CGTA 1979 s.86)

Like the relief for exchanges, the relief for reconstructions and amalgamations involves two companies A and B. But whereas with exchanges, Company A acquires the shares of Company B, in a reconstruction or amalgamation it acquires company B's business. The consideration, however, goes not to Company B, but to its shareholders, and takes the form of an issue of shares or debentures by Company A. The shares in Company B are either retained or liquidated.

The terms 'reconstruction' and 'amalgamation' are not defined in the CGT legislation. The classic definitions were given by Buckley J in *Re South African Supply and Cold Storage Company* [1904] 2 Ch 268. In a reconstruction Company B is a new company with substantially the same shareholders as Company A formed to carry on substantially the same business. In an amalgamation the pre-existing undertakings of two or more companies are brought together in Company A. Company A may be newly formed for the purpose, or it may be one of the pre-existing companies. After the amalgamation, its shareholders must include substantially all the former shareholders of the pre-existing companies. Reconstructions and amalgamations are effected either under Companies Act 1985 s.427 or in a liquidation under Insolvency Act 1986 s.110.

Strictly the division of a company's undertaking into two or more companies owned by different sets of shareholders (for example family groups) is not a reconstruction. But the Revenue so treat such exercises provided that the division of the undertaking is a segregation of trades or businesses and not merely a division of assets (SP5/85).

Reconstructions and amalgamations, and divisions treated as reconstructions, can all involve the disposal of assets from the old compan(ies) to the new. Such disposals are treated as no gain/no loss disposals (TA 1970 s.267). But for this treatment to apply, both companies must be UK resident and the old company must not receive any consideration for the transfer.

Motive test (CGTA1979 ss.87-88)

Some of the transactions described in this chapter are subject to a motive test. The transactions which are so subject are share-for-share exchanges, reconstructions and amalgamations, and divisions treated as reconstructions.

A transaction falling in one of these categories does not enjoy relief unless:

(a) it is effected for bona fide commercial reasons; and
(b) it does not form part of a scheme or arrangements of which the main purpose, or one of the main purposes, is the avoidance of liability to CGT or corporation tax.

This motive test was enacted as a result of schemes exemplified in *Floor v Davis* [1980] AC 695 and *Furniss v Dawson* [1984] STC 153. Under such schemes, shareholders about to sell a company would form an offshore company and effect a share-for-share exchange with that company. The offshore company would then sell the original company, and CGT would be deferred or, in an extension of the scheme, avoided.

The motive test does not apply to shareholders who own less than 5 per cent of the target company. A clearance procedure exists and should be used in all cases. Points to note include the following:

(1) The Revenue do sometimes refuse clearance where the proposed consideration on a share-for-share exchange is short-dated stock rather than cash, as this normally has little discernible commercial purpose. However clearance is normally forthcoming where the stock has a life of more than six months.
(2) In considering a clearance application, the Revenue do not necessarily indicate whether the other conditions for relief

are satisfied, but if it is obvious that those conditions will not be met, they say so.

Demergers (FA 1980 s.117 and Sch 18)

Three types of demerger do not count as a distribution for income tax purposes if certain conditions are met (TA 1988 ss.213-18). The following demergers are so treated:

Type 1 The transfer of shares in a 75 per cent subsidiary to the members of the parent company ('the distributing company').

Type 2 The transfer of a trade by the distributing company to another company which in return issues its own shares to the distributing company's members.

Type 3 The transfer by the distributing comany of the shares in a 75 per cent subsidiary to another company which issues shares to the distributing company's members.

Strictly none of these types of demerger qualifies for the reliefs described in this chapter, for they are transactions of a wholly different nature. But a demerger of the first kind is deemed to be a reorganisation (FA 1980 Sch 17 para 9), with the result that it does not count as a capital distribution triggering a part disposal by the shareholders. Unfortunately, this treatment does not exempt gains accruing to the distributing company on this kind of demerger, and so, if the shares concerned show a gain, that form of demerger has a CGT cost.

In practice the other two kinds of demerger are treated as reconstructions (SP 5/85), the shares distributed in a demerger of the third kind being treated as an identifiable part of the distributing company's undertaking. This means that so far as the shareholders are concerned, the shares in the distributing company are treated as original shares, and those in the recipient company as a new holding. The disposal by the distributing company is treated as a no gain/no loss disposal (TA 1970 s.267).

VI Foreign Element

Chapter 22
Territorial Limits

Introduction

A person is only liable to capital gains tax if he is resident or ordinarily resident in the UK. In this respect, CGT differs from income tax, for that tax is chargeable either if the taxpayer resides in the UK or if the source of the income is situate here.

Residence (CGTA 1979 ss.18 and 52)

The residence of individuals and companies is determined by the same tests as apply for income and corporation tax. Trusts, however are subject to special rules enacted specifically for the purposes of CGT.

Individual residence is a question of fact which, in practice, is largely governed by published Revenue practice (IR 20, paras 6-30). An individual is regarded as UK resident if he is present in the UK for more than six months in any year of assessment, if his visits over several years average more than three months per year, or if he has available accommodation here. The latter is most important in practice, but it may be disregarded if the individual works full-time abroad (TA 1988 s.335).

Company residence now turns in the first instance on where the company is registered (FA 1988 s.66). If the company is registered abroad, the common law central management and control test applies: the company resides wherever the central management and control of its business abides (*De Beers Consolidated Mines Ltd v Howe* [1906] AC 455). Normally central management and control abides with the directors, but if they are mere cyphers for the shareholders, the residence of the shareholders can determine the company's residence (*Unit Construction Co Ltd v Bullock* [1960] AC 351).

A UK registered company which first carries on business after 15 March 1988 is ipso facto resident in the UK. There are now

Territorial limits

no circumstances in which such a company can be or become non-resident.

The residence of UK registered companies which commenced business before 15 March 1988 is somewhat complex (FA 1988 Sch 7). If the company became non-resident under a specific Treasury consent, it can remain non-resident so long as it carries on business. If the company became non-resident under one of the general Treasury consents, it can only remain non-resident so long as it is taxable abroad. All other UK companies which are non-resident under the central management and control test can remain so until 15 March 1993, when they will automatically become resident.

A trust is non-resident for CGT purposes if all or a majority of the trustees are non-resident, and the general administration of the trust is carried on abroad (CGTA 1979 s.52). A trustee is treated as non-resident if he is a professional trustee and the settlor was neither resident nor domiciled in the UK when he made the settlement. If in such a case all the trustees are, or are treated as, non-resident, the general administration of the trusts is treated as carried on abroad.

UK branch or agency (CGTA 1979 s.12; TA 1988 s.11; FA 1989 ss.126-34)

There is one exception to the rule that non-residents are not charged to CGT. This arises where the non-resident is trading in the UK through a branch or agency. In these circumstances, gains arising on certain UK assets are taxable. Assets so charged are assets used for the purposes of the trade and assets used or acquired for use by the branch or agency.

At one time this charge on non-residents was easy to avoid, for it did not apply once the asset was removed abroad or after the year of assessment in which the branch or agency trade ceased. These avoidance possibilities ceased to be available on 14 March 1989. A branch or agency asset removed abroad after that date is deemed to be disposed of at market value and a market value deemed disposal of all branch or agency assets takes place on the cessation of any branch or agency trade.

Roll-over relief also used to offer a means of avoiding the branch or agency charge (for roll-over relief see chapter 19). The relief applied on the disposal of branch or agency assets even if the new asset was situated outside the UK and thus outside the charge to CGT. This avoidance was stopped with effect from 14 March 1989 and now roll-over relief only applies if the new asset is a branch or agency asset.

Until 14 March 19898, the branch or agency charge applied only to those trading in the UK. Now, however, it is extended to the branches and agencies of foreign professions and vocations. But the charge is not retrospective, for all assets used in such branches or agencies are deemed to have been disposed of and reacquired at market value immediately before 14 March 1989. They thus have a tax-free updated base value.

Migration

Individuals and trusts have always been free to migrate. Migration does not occasion a charge to CGT, save insofar as the migrant has been the recipient of an asset in respect of which a hold-over relief election has been made (see p 111). The migration of a trust can also trigger a CGT charge if a beneficiary has previously disposed of his beneficial interest (see p 146).

Strictly, CGT is payable if the individual or trust has been resident in the UK at any time during the year of assessment in which the migration occurs. In law, therefore, it it necessary for a migrant to wait until 6 April following his migration before realising any gains. But in practice a relaxation is made for individuals who are permanently giving up UK residence. So long as their non-resident status is established, they are treated as non-resident from the moment of departure (Concession D2).

Foreign registered companies can now migrate, for TA 1970 s.482, the section which used to make company migration without Treasury consent an offence, no longer applies. Migration is effected by simply moving central management and control from the UK to some foreign territory. But if this is done, all the company's assets are deemed to be disposed of at market value (FA 1988 s.105). A further consequence is that the right to claim roll-over relief is lost to the extent that the old assets were disposed of before the migration and the new assets are acquired thereafter.

Exceptions to the migration charge are made if the company's assets continue to be used in a UK branch or agency. Relief may also be given if the migrating company is a 75 per cent subsidiary of a UK resident parent. Here the net gain accruing on the migration may be postponed, and it becomes assessable on the parent if and insofar as the migrant disposes of its assets during the next six years. The parent is also assessable if the migrant ceases at anytime to be its subsidiary (FA 1988 s.107).

Territorial limits

The remittance basis (CGTA 1979 s.14)

The remittance basis applies to individuals who are not domiciled in the UK. It cannot apply either to trusts or to companies. Domicile is determined by the general common law rules, and there is no concept of deemed domicile such as applies to inheritance tax (IHTA 1984 s.267). Proposals are being mooted to reform the law of domicile, but so far these have not been enacted (see Law Commission report no. 168, September 1987).

The remittance basis applies only to gains accruing on assets situate outside the UK. In general, the CGT rules for determining the situs of assets follow those of the common law (CGTA 1979 s.18). But one notable exception is that a debt is situate in the UK if the creditor resides here. Prima facie this means that the foreign bank accounts of non-domiciliaries can never be situate in the UK, but an exception is made for foreign bank accounts denominated in a foreign currency (CGTA 1979 s.18(4)(j); see further SP 10/84).

Under the remittance basis, gains accruing on foreign assets are not charged save insofar as amounts are received in the UK in respect of those gains. Money is treated as received in the UK if it is paid used or enjoyed in the UK, or if it is in any manner or form brought here. Gains applied in settling foreign indebtedness are also treated as remitted to the UK if the money originally borrowed is brought here (TA 1988 s.65(6)-(8)).

Whether a gain has been remitted is a question of fact. In practice, remittances from the proceeds of disposal of an asset are treated as remittances of gain and base cost in proportion to the total amounts of the gain and base cost. Separate bank accounts may be used to avoid the remittance of gains if one account is used for the proceeds of assets disposed of at a gain, and the second for other disposals. Remittances from the latter will not be remittances of gains.

Delayed remittances (CGTA 1979 s.13)

Companies, trusts, and domiciled individuals are entitled to relief if, through no fault of their own, the remittance of a foreign gain is delayed. For this relief to apply it must be shown that:

(1) the taxpayer was unable to transfer the gain to the UK;
(2) the inability was due to the laws of the territory where the gain arose, or to the executive action of its government,

or to the impossibility of obtaining foreign currency there; and

(3) the inability was not due to any want of reasonable endeavours on the part of the taxpayer.

If a gain satisfies these conditions, the amount of the gain is deducted from the amount on which the taxpayer is assessed to capital gains tax for the year in which it arose. The gain becomes chargeable if and at such time as the conditions ceased to be satisfied. The relief does not apply unless it is claimed within six years of the year of assessment in which the gain originally accrued

Double taxation relief (CGTA 1979 s.10)

Many countries tax non-residents in respect of capital gains accruing on assets situate within their territory. As a result, UK residents owning assets in the country concerned face two lots of tax, one in the country where the asset is situate and the second in the UK.

In practice double taxation of the same gain is avoided. If a double tax treaty exists between the foreign country and the UK, the matter is regulated by the treaty. Most treaties to which the UK is a party are based on the OECD Draft Convention of 1963 and the OECD Model Convention of 1977. As such they give the UK sole taxing rights on all gains save those arising from land in the foreign country, a permanent establishment there, or a fixed base for performing independent personal services. Tax charged by the foreign country in respect of those gains is allowed as a credit against the UK CGT.

Where there is no treaty between the UK and the foreign country, unilateral relief applies under UK domestic legislation (TA 1988 s.790). This relief also takes the form of credit relief, allowing tax charged by the foreign country as a credit against the UK CGT. Whether credit relief applies by treaty or unilaterally, it cannot exceed the UK tax otherwise chargeable on the gain (TA 1988 ss.796 and 797).

Because non-residents are not liable to UK CGT, non-residents rarely find themselves concerned both with UK CGT and with CGT in their own country. Such a situation only arises where the foreigner is liable to UK CGT because he is trading here through a branch or agency. In these circumstances, the UK almost always has taxing rights, for even if a treaty applies, the branch or agency is a permanent establishment or a fixed base

Territorial limits

for performing independent personal services. Where a treaty applies, the foreign country will be required to give relief for any UK CGT by credit or by exemption. If there is no treaty, relief is a matter for the domestic tax code of the foreign country.

Dual residents

A dual resident may be defined as a person who is resident in the UK for UK tax purposes and resident in a foreign country under the tax law of that country. Where a double tax treaty exists between the UK and the foreign country, the treaty lays down rules for determining which country the taxpayer is resident in for the purposes of a treaty. Where under the treaty he is resident in the foreign country he is in the curious position of being foreign resident where the treaty applies and otherwise UK resident. He may be described as dual resident under a treaty.

Persons who are dual resident under a treaty are now subject to specific provisions in the CGT code:

(1) Hold-over relief for gifts is not available if the recipient is dual resident under a treaty and a claw-back occurs if the recipient is not dual resident when the gift is made but becomes so subsequently. If the recipient is a company, these consequences apply if the shareholders are or become dual resident (CGTA 1979 ss.126A(2), 126B(3), 126C(9), and 147B(2); FA 1986 s.58). These restrictions to hold-over relief do not apply if and so long as the gifted asset is an asset such as UK land over which the treaty gives the UK taxing rights.

(2) A company which becomes dual resident under a treaty is deemed to dispose of all assets exempted from CGT by the treaty (FA 1988 s.106). It is also unable to claim roll-over relief in so far as the new assets are exempted from CGT by the treaty. These provisions correspond to those applying when a company becomes non-resident under UK domestic law, and the same deferral applies if the company is the subsidiary of a UK parent (see p 135).

(3) A company which is already dual resident under a treaty suffers a deemed disposal on the occasion of any asset becoming exempt under the treaty (FA 1989 s. 132). This normally happens when a permanent establishment closes or movables are removed abroad. Roll-over relief is not available where the new assets are exempt from CGT under the treaty (ibid s.133).

Chapter 23

Shareholders in Non-Resident Companies

Introduction

Non-resident companies are not subject to CGT, for they count as separate entities, and, by being non-resident, they are beyond the territorial scope of the tax. Certain non-resident companies offer a complete shelter from CGT, in that their gains cannot be attributed back to UK shareholders. Other companies, by contrast, are subject to apportionment, and, if certain conditions are met, their gains can be attributed to the shareholders.

Companies subject to apportionment (CGTA 1979 s.15)

The companies subject to apportionment are those which would be close companies if they were resident in the UK. The term 'close company' has the same meaning as for income tax purposes. The basis of the definition is that a company is close if it is controlled by five or fewer participators, but exceptions are made where more than 35 per cent of the shares are held by the public, and where the company is in a group whose ultimate parent is open (TA 1988 ss.414 and 415).

In practice the definition of close company means that any non-resident subsidiary of a quoted company is unlikely to be subject to apportionment. The position is otherwise if the non-resident company is directly owned by individuals or trustees, or if it is a member of a privately owned group.

The apportionment (CGTA 1979 s.15)

An apportionment is made whenever a chargeable gain accrues to the non-resident company. The apportionment is made to each shareholder on the basis of the proportion of the company's assets to which he would be entitled if the company were liquidated.

A shareholder is chargeable on the gain apportioned to him if two conditions are satisfied:

(1) the gain apportioned to him is more than 5 per cent of the total gain realised by the company, and
(2) the shareholder is resident in the UK, and, if he is an individual, domiciled here as well.

Gains accruing to the non-resident company are not reduced by any allowable losses. But such losses can be apportioned to the shareholders, and the shareholders may then set them against gains apportioned in the same year from the same or any other non-resident company. But the losses cannot be carried forward, and nor can they be set against the shareholder's general gains.

Reliefs (CGTA 1979 s.15(5))

The following gains are excepted from apportionment:

(1) any gain distributed by the company to the shareholders or creditors within two years from the time when it accrued to the company;
(2) any gain accruing on the disposal of tangible assets used and used only for the purposes of a trade carried on by the company wholly outside the UK;
(3) any gain accruing on the disposal of foreign currency or a foreign bank account, where the money is used for the purposes of a trade carried on by the company wholly outside the UK;
(4) any gain accruing to a UK branch or agency in respect of which the company is itself chargeable to tax (see p 134).

If the company is resident in a territory with which the UK has a Double Tax Treaty, the treaty will normally give that territory sole taxing rights over the gain (see p 137). The better view is that such treaties prevent attribution of the gain to any UK shareholders, and this, it is understood, is accepted by the Revenue.

Double taxation (CGTA 1979 s.15(7))

The attribution of gains to shareholders prima facie results in double taxation. The shareholder is taxed on his share of the gain when it accrues to the company, and subsequently, when he disposes of his shares, the gain on which he is then taxed includes the earlier corporate gain. This double taxation is relieved to a limited extent, for tax paid on the apportioned gain is deducted in computing the gain on the shares. But this relief is not a deduction of tax and from tax and as a result, substantial double taxation remains.

It is open to a non-resident company to pay any CGT charged on its shareholders. Where this happens, such payment does not count as a distribution for income tax or CGT purposes.

Non-resident groups (CGTA 1979 s.16)

If several non-resident companies would count as a group for CGT purposes if they were resident, intra group disposals count as no gain/no loss disposals. But for these purposes such groups exclude any UK resident company which would otherwise be a group member.

Should the non-resident company realising the gain be a subsidiary of another non-resident, the gain is apportioned to that non-resident and treated as accruing to it. This apportionment can go on through any number of non-resident companies until the ultimate shareholders are reached.

Trustee shareholders (FA 1981 s.85)

Until 10 March 1981 the inter-position of a non-resident trust between a non-resident company and its UK resident owners avoided the attribution of the company's gains, for the only gains which could be attributed to the beneficiaries of a non-resident trust were those actually realised by the trustees. In respect of gains accruing to a non-resident company after 10 March 1981 this has been changed. From that date the persons treated as if a chargeable gain accruing to the company had accrued to them include non-resident trustees. Any gain so apportioned to trustees counts as a trust gain, able to be attributed to beneficiaries who receive capital payments (see p 142).

Chapter 24

Beneficiaries under Non-Resident Trusts

Introduction

Since CGT is not charged on non-residents, non-resident trusts offer scope for avoidance. These avoidance possibilities may be enjoyed by both fixed-interest and discretionary trusts, for both forms of trust count as separate entities for CGT purposes (see chapter 12). But the avoidance possibilities are curtailed by rules which require trust gains to be attributed to resident beneficiaries who receive capital payments.

Attribution of trust gains (FA 1981 s.80)

In each year of assessment, a computation is made of the gains of the trustees which would have been chargeable had the trust been resident in the UK. In computing these gains, account may be taken of allowable losses and the gains so ascertained, together with gains from previous years not already attributed to beneficiaries, are called 'the trust gains for the year'. The trust gains for the year are attributed to beneficiaries who receive capital payments from the trustees in that year, or have received such payments at any earlier time after 10 March 1981.

In computing the trust gains, the losses which may be taken into account are not merely those of the current year, but unrelieved losses of all previous years in which the settlement was non-resident (FA 1981 s.83(6)). The losses so allowed include unrelieved losses accruing before 6 April 1981, but the trust gains cannot include gains realised before then.

Trust gains are attributed to the beneficiaries in proportion to the amount of capital payments received by them, but the attribution may not exceed the payments. A capital payment is left out of account for the purpose of attribution to the extent that it has already been taken into account in an earlier year. Thus two notional cumulative funds are created, and carried forward from year to year, one consisting of trust gains and the other of capital payments. The latter, less the total gains already attributed to the beneficiaries are charged to tax to the extent that they are matched by the accumulated gains, reduced by any which have already been attributed.

Territorial limits (FA 1981 s.80)

There can be no trust gains for a year of assessment unless the settlor was both resident and domiciled in the UK either in that year or when he made the settlement. It is accepted that a dead settlor has neither a residence nor a domicile and so, once the settlor is dead, it is only his residence and domicile when he made the settlement which are material. These rules mean that a settlement cannot be subject to the attribution of gains if the settlor has always been non-domiciled, and so non-resident settlements which are excluded property settlement for IHT purposes never suffer attribution of gains and thus are a complete CGT shelter.

Gains attributed to a beneficiary are not taxable unless he is domiciled in the UK at some time during the year of attribution. Nor is the beneficiary liable if he is neither resident nor ordinarily resident, for, although any capital payments will cause chargeable gains to accrue to him, he will not be chargeable to tax on general principles. Settlements where some of the beneficiaries are non-resident or non-domiciled thus offer considerable scope for avoiding CGT, for capital payments to such beneficiaries reduce trust gains without resulting in a liability to tax.

Example

Tom, Dick, Harry and Bert are all beneficiaries of a non-resident settlement made by a settlor resident and domiciled in the UK. All were resident in the United Kingdom, but Tom was domiciled in France throughout the relevant years of assessment. The trustees' gains and capital payments made to the beneficiaries were as follows:

	Gains	Tom	Dick	Harry	Bert
1985-86	£2,000	£500	nil	nil	nil
1986-87	£9,000	£500	£ 500	£ 500	£ 500
1987-88	£1,500	nil	£3,000	£3,000	£3,000

The trust gains attributed are as follows:

	Gains	Tom	Dick	Harry	Bert
1985-6					
Trust gains	£ 2,000				

Beneficiaries under non-resident trusts

Attributed	£ 500	£500	nil	nil	nil
Carried forward	£ 1,500				
1986-7					
Gains brought forward	£ 1,500				
Gains of year	£ 9,000				
Trust gains	£10,500				
Attributed	£ 2,000	£500	£500	£500	£500
Carried forward	£ 8,500				
1987-8					
Gains brought forward	£ 8,500				
Gains of year	£ 1,500				
Trust gains	£10,000				
Attributed	£ 9,000	nil	£3,000	£3,000	£3,000
Carried forward	£ 1,000				

Although Tom has £1,000 trust gains attributed to him he is not charged to tax thereon because he was domiciled outside the UK throughout the years in which the gains accrued. The others are charged on the gains attributed to them in the appropriate years, but in the example their gains are within their annual exemption and if they had no other gains they would not be charged.

Capital payments (FA 1981 s.83)

A capital payment is any payment not chargeable to income tax on the beneficiary. In the case of a beneficiary who is neither resident nor ordinarily resident in the United Kingdom, it is any payment received otherwise than as income. The term also includes the transfer of an asset or the conferring of any benefit, as well as any occasion on which settled property becomes nominee property (see p 72).

A beneficiary is treated as receiving a capital payment from the trustees if:

(a) he receives it from them directly or indirectly;
(b) it is applied by the trustees in payment of his debts;
(c) it is applied by them for his benefit; or
(d) it is received by a third person at the beneficiary's direction.

Transfers between settlements (FA 1981 s.82)

If the capital payment is an outright payment of money the amount of the payment is the money paid. Where assets other than money are transferred, or where there is merely a loan, the assets or the loan have to be valued and the capital payment is treated as equal to the value of the benefit conferred. In the case of a loan, therefore, the capital payment is the value of the loan and not the money lent. But demand loans are not treated in this way, and the Revenue normally treat the interest foregone as a benefit in each year during which the loan is outstanding.

Migrating settlements (FA 1981 s.82)

The attribution of gains to beneficiaries does not apply to gains accruing while a settlement is resident. But a capital payment made by a resident settlement can be taken into account if it is made in contemplation of the settlement becoming non-resident. Such a payment will result in a gain accruing to the beneficiary as and when the trust becomes non-resident and realises gains.

If a non-resident settlement becomes resident, any outstanding trust gains are not wiped off the slate. They can be attributed to beneficiaries after the settlement becomes resident, the attribution being by capital payments in the normal way.

Transfers between settlements (FA 1981 s.82)

Where the trustees of one settlement transfer the settled property to another settlement, the outstanding trust gains of the transferor settlement are transferred to the transferee settlement, or, if part only of the settled property is transferred, a proportionate part of those gains is transferred. The outstanding trust gains are the trust gains of the transferor settlement for the year of the transfer, as reduced by any gains attributed to beneficiaries in that year.

These rules apply not merely where both settlements are non-resident but also where one or both is resident. If the transferor settlement is resident, the outstanding trust gains are any gains from the non-resident period not already attributed to beneficiaries. If the transferee settlement is resident or becomes so in the year of the transfer, the outstanding gains transferred to it are treated as if they had accrued to it during a non-resident period prior to the transfer.

Beneficial interests under non-resident settlements (FA 1981 s.88)

The exemption for disposals of beneficial interests (p 74) does not apply if the trustees of the settlement are non-resident when the disposal takes place. But this does not apply to the notional disposal which takes place when the beneficiary becomes absolutely entitled to the settled property.

Where a benefical interest in a resident settlement is disposed of and the trustees subsequently become non-resident, any gain accruing on the disposal of the beneficial interest which was exempt is deemed to accrue to and be chargeable on the trustees immediately prior to the trust becoming non-resident. This charge is only avoided if the trustees have disposed of all the assets which were in the settlement when the disposal of the beneficial interest took place. The chargeable gain accruing to the trustees cannot exceed the market value of the assets which they have retained since the disposal of the beneficial interest. If the trustees fail to pay any tax due within twelve months of its becoming payable, the Revenue can assess the beneficiary who originally disposed of the beneficial interest. But such an assessment may only be made within six years of disposal and the beneficiary is entitled to recover any tax paid from the trustees.

The charge on the disposal of a beneficial interest can be penal, for an original beneficiary under a settlement has no acquisition cost. This arises because there is no corresponding disposal when he acquires his interest; the only disposal is by the settlor to the trustees and that is of the settled property. Accordingly market value is not substituted on the beneficiary's acquisition (see p 17). The result is that the entire value of the beneficial interest at the time of its disposal is chargeable gain. Since these rules apply as much on gifts as on sales, even the release of an interest under a non-resident trust can occasion a charge, unable to be held over if the reversioner is non-resident.

Inadvertent liabilities under these rules can be avoided by ensuring that beneficial interests have no value. This result naturally follows with a discretionary trust and otherwise may be achieved by making beneficial interests subject to revocation or overriding powers of appointment.

VII Tax Planning

Chapter 25

Personal Planning

Sheltering substantial gains

The most common situation in which CGT planning is required is where the taxpayer is about to dispose of a single substantial asset. Typical examples are the sale or flotation of a private company, or the sale of land.

In situations of this kind, the first stage in any tax planning exercise is to see how big any chargeable gain will really be. With many long-held assets, the combined effect of 1982 rebasing and indexation is to eliminate the gain or make it a relatively small proportion of the proceeds of disposal. If the gain is 25 per cent or less of the proceeds, tax will be less than 10 per cent, and this may be regarded as acceptable.

Tax planning becomes necessary if even after indexation and rebasing, the gain is substantial. A point which cannot be emphasised too strongly is that a taxpayer in this situation can avoid the tax. All he needs to do is become non-resident before effecting the disposal. Strictly, he needs to be non-resident throughout the year of the disposal, but by concession the Revenue backdate the period of non-residence to the date of departure (see p 135). It is normally considered wise to remain non-resident for at least three years, for CGT is only avoided if the taxpayer ceases to be both resident and ordinarily resident in the UK. But recent cases have indicated that absence for only a single tax year can be sufficient, provided the taxpayer establishes a permanent place of residence abroad (*Reed v Clark* [1985] STC 323).

In some cases, a taxpayer about to realise a large gain may be willing to migrate in the future, but not immediately. In certain cases, he can avoid tax by deferring the gain until he is non-resident. In the case of shares this can be done if the purchaser is another company prepared to issue shares or debentures rather than pay cash (see p 126). With land, this deferral may be achieved if the land is compulsorily purchased, and a roll-over relief claim

Personal planning

is established by investing the proceeds in new land. In both cases, the deferral is not clawed back when the taxpayer subsequently becomes non-resident and sells the new asset tax-free.

Where a taxpayer is unwilling or unable to consider non-residence, tax can still be avoided, but only by not selling the asset. Sooner or later all individual taxpayers do achieve a new tax-free base value, for this happens automatically on death (p 101). This new base value is not of great interest to the taxpayer himself, but it benefits his family, for the funds passing to them will not previously have been depleted by CGT.

Assuming retention until death is not attractive, the only remaining method of offsetting a chargeable gain is by loss relief. Unfortunately, only capital losses may be relieved against capital gains, and they must either be realised in the same year of assessment or carried forward from previous years (see p 5). When a substantial gain is in prospect, taxpayers should consider realising assets showing a loss at the same time.

Long-term planning

It has to be admitted that the steps required to offset an imminent gain are dramatic. Matters are altogether easier if CGT planning is thought about when the asset is acquired or when it is not showing a gain. In these circumstances, one well-recognised vehicle exists to shelter long-term CGT liabilities, namely the non-resident trust.

A trust counts as a non-resident for CGT purposes if all or a majority of the trustees are non-resident and the general administration of the trust is carried on abroad (see p 71). Since it is non-resident, such a trust does not attract CGT. This is so whether the trust is fixed-interest, discretionary or accumulation and maintenance. It is even possible for the settlor to be a beneficiary, for the rules attributing gains to the settlor do not apply to the non-resident trusts (see p74).

The one disadvantage of non-resident trusts is that capital payments to resident beneficiaries do attract CGT. In theory, this can increase CGT, for the beneficiary may pay tax at 40 per cent whereas a resident trust is taxed at 25 or 35 per cent (see p 73). But this disadvantage is more apparent than real, for capital does not have to be advanced out of the trust, and instead the beneficiaries can enjoy the income of a fund that has not been diminished by CGT. The chances are that some beneficiaries will sooner or later become non-resident and when this happens capital payments to them do not attract tax (see p 143).

Where the settlor wishes to retain the income of the assets he is settling, he can be the initial life tenant. Should he wish to divest himself of the assets for IHT or other reasons, the ideal form of trust is an accumulation or maintenance trust for children or grandchildren. Such a trust should confer life rather than absolute interests so as to avoid unnecessary deemed disposals (see p 72).

Initially resident trusts

Many individuals are uneasy about non-resident trusts, for the setting-up and running costs can be considerable, and the trustees are usually strangers situate in a low tax jurisdiction outside the UK. For these individuals the solution is to create a resident trust, which becomes non-resident only when the gain is about to be realised. Provided non-residence is achieved in the year of assessment prior to that in which the gain is realised, CGT on the gains will be avoided in the same way as with settlements which were non-resident at the outset (see p 135).

A trust becomes non-resident if non-residents are appointed to be trustees in place of the UK trustees, and the general administration of the trust is transferred abroad. Where the proper law of the trust is English, it is normally not proper to appoint non-residents to be trustees unless there is express power to do so (*Re Whitehead* [1971] 2 All ER 1334). For this reason, all trusts should include such a power. In the absence of a power of this kind, an appointment of non-resident trustees would not be invalid, but if the non-resident trustees defaulted, the retiring UK trustees who concurred in the improper appointment could be held liable for any ensuing loss to the trust fund.

It is also necessary to ensure that the non-resident trustees include at least two individuals, for trustees retiring from an English trust do not get a good discharge unless they are replaced by at least two individuals or a trust corporation (Trustee Act 1925 s.37(1)(c)). It is widely thought that this rule can be displaced by express provision in the trust deed, but the point is not free of doubt and so it is better to err on the side of caution and see that in all cases at least two individuals are appointed. The consequence of the retiring trustees not getting a good discharge is that they remain trustees, with the probable result that the majority of the trustees will not be non-resident, thereby causing the trust to retain its UK residence for CGT purposes.

Personal planning

The migration of a trust currently does not occasion a deemed disposal of the trust assets. Such a charge was widely expected to be introduced in the 1989 Budget, but this did not happen. There are, however, two other tax points to watch on migration. First, a beneficiary who has received a capital payment in anticipation of the migration becomes taxable on the payment as and when the non-resident trustees realise gains (see p 145). Second, a charge is imposed if a beneficiary has previously disposed of his beneficial interest, and the trustees have not in the meantime sold all the assets then in the trust (see p 146).

Assets showing a gain

So far it has been assumed that assets are transferred into a settlement on acquisition or when they are not showing a gain. In the real world many taxpayers do not think about CGT planning until the asset is already showing a gain. In these circumstances, the taxpayer's objective is to shelter any future gain, without triggering an immediate liability on the gain that has accrued already. Typically, this problem arises with shares in private companies where flotation is anticipated in the medium term, or with land which may in due course be zoned for development.

The best advice to the taxpayer in these circumstances is often to do nothing. If the taxpayer is elderly, a new base value will be obtained if he dies prior to the sale of the asset, and this will wipe out both the accrued and the future gain. Otherwise, it is always open to the taxpayer to become non-resident prior to the realisation of the gain, and here too tax will be avoided on both the accrued and the future gain.

Where such advice was impractical or unacceptable, general hold-over relief used to offer a solution (see p 107). The asset could be transferred into a resident settlement, and the immediate tax charge would be avoided by a hold-over election. In the year of assessment prior to any sale, the trust would migrate. Such migration triggered a charge on the held-over gain (see p 111), but the subsequent gain was tax-free. Such a trust was commonly referred to as a freezer trust.

Freezer trusts can still be used in this way if the trust is a discretionary trust or if the assets are business assets within CGTA s.126, for in those circumstances hold-over relief is still available (see chapter 18). But it may be questioned how worthwhile freezer trusts really are, for once the asset is transferred into the trust, the held-over gain is locked in. The opportunity of avoiding tax on that gain by the settlor dying or becoming non-resident has been lost.

Where hold-over relief is now not available, freezer trusts are very unlikely to be worthwhile, for the transfer of the asset into the trust will occasion an immediate CGT charge. Such a charge is usually too high a price for avoiding tax on a future gain which might not materialise, and which could in any event be sheltered by the death or non-residence of the settlor.

Portfolio investors

Although sophisticated CGT planning revolves around single assets showing a substantial gain, most individual taxpayers only become concerned with CGT when they switch assets in their investment portfolios. For these taxpayers, the basic rule is to balance gains and losses and see that the net gains of any year of assessment do not exceed the basic annual exemption. Indexation and rising inflation mean this is currently not a difficult objective to attain.

Portfolio investors can face difficulties when a company in which they hold shares is the subject of a successful take-over bid, for such a bid normally results in a substantial uplift in the price of its shares. But in most cases, the adverse CGT consequences of this can be avoided in that shares or loan-stock are usually offered as an alternative to cash. If the taxpayer elects to take this alternative, the new shares or loan-stock are treated as the same asset as the old, and deferral is achieved (see p 126).

Portfolio investors should always remember that some forms of investment are exempt. Gilts and qualifying corporate bonds are the prime examples, but these are now of little practical importance, for indexation means that they are rarely disposed of at a gain. Much greater significance attaches to BES shares and shares in personal equity plans.

The Business Expansion Scheme was originally introduced as an income shelter, and as such it remains. But since 1986 gains on BES shares have also been exempt from CGT (see p 89). Now that income tax and CGT rates are at the same level, this aspect of the Business Expansion Scheme is increasingly important.

Many private investors have rather looked down on PEPs and it is indeed true that the annual amount which may be invested is still only £4,800. But there is no limit to the amount by which the initial investment may grow, and any gains are exempt (see

Personal planning

p 90). PEPs have a particular attraction in 1989, for the taxpayer may take out a £3,000 plan under the old 1986 Reglations, and a new plan under the 1989 Regulations.

Spreading assets round the family

From 6 April 1990, the income and gains of spouses will be taxed separately. This means married couples will each be entitled to a £5,000 annual exemption and to a 25 per cent basic-rate band (see p 60). Disposals between spouses will, however, remain no gain/no loss disposals, and they will also be free of any inheritance tax charge because of the IHT spouse exemption.

In broad terms, it will clearly be tax-effective for spouses to equalise their assets. This is particularly true of portfolio investors, for the doubling-up of the annual exemption may obviate the modest CGT charge which would otherwise be due.

The annual exemption and basic-rate band will be available to a spouse even if he or she acquired the asset generating the gain from the other spouse, and that spouse has already utilised his exemption and basic-rate band. For that reason, CGT will be able to be reduced by transferring investments between spouses prior to a disposal. The only limitation is the *Ramsay* principle, but this will not be in issue if the transfer is effected before the disposal is definitely decided on (*Craven v White* [1988] STC 476).

Spreading assets around other members of the family can also be effective, for if the recipients are of modest means, annual exemptions and basic-rate bands will be available. But here the necessary spreading needs to be done when the assets are first acquired or when they are not showing a gain. If gifts are delayed until a gain has already accrued, the abolition of general hold-over relief means the gain has to be charged on the donor rather than being carried forward to the recipient.

Inheritance tax planning and CGT

To some extent there is a conflict between prudent inheritance tax planning and prudent CGT planning. The correct IHT strategy is to make lifetime gifts to other individuals or to fixed-interest or accumulation and maintenance trusts. Such gifts are potentially exempt (IHTA 1984 s.3A), and IHT is avoided provided the donor survives seven years.

Inheritance tax planning and CGT

Gifts of this sort are entirely satisfactory from a CGT standpoint where the gifted property is cash, exempt assets, or assets not showing a gain. But where the gift is of an asset showing a gain, there is a conflict between IHT and CGT, for the ending of general hold-over relief means the gift will normally occasion an immediate CGT charge, such as would have been avoided had the donor retained the asset until death. In some cases, this CGT charge can almost equal the IHT the gift is intended to avoid, as where the asset has only a nominal base cost. Furthermore, if the donor fails to survive seven years, not even the advantage of avoiding IHT is obtained. Thus, in extreme circumstances, an inter vivos gift can occasion both 40 per cent CGT and 40 per cent IHT.

In broad terms these considerations constitute a compelling argument for restricting inter vivos gifts to assets which are not showing a gain. To some extent business assets which still qualify for hold-over relief represent an exception. But gifts of such assets still carry the disadvantage that whereas hold-over relief merely defers a gain, retention until death eliminates it. In the case of business property and farmland, business and agricultural property relief may reduce any IHT on death to 20 per cent, and so the effect of a gift of business assets with nominal base value may be to preserve a latent liability to CGT at 40 per cent at the cost of avoiding IHT at 20 per cent. For this reason, even with hold-over relief, gifts of assets showing a latent gain are best avoided in IHT planning.

Chapter 26

Business Planning

Introduction

For individuals and partnerships the fundamentals of business planning are the same as those applicable to personal tax. In the last analysis, CGT is a voluntary tax, for assets need not be sold, a new base value is obtained on death, and tax-free gains may be realised if the taxpayer discontinues the business and subsequently becomes non-resident. A further relief of increasing value is retirement relief (see chapter 16).

The fundamentals for companies are not so favourable, for companies can neither die nor retire. UK registered companies cannot migrate, and foreign companies can only migrate at the cost of a deemed disposal of all their assets (see p 135). But companies do enjoy one advantage over individuals, for net gains can be set against trading losses and management expenses (see p 64). Relief against trading losses is only available in respect of the losses of the current and the next succeeding accounting periods, but surplus management expenses can be carried forward indefinitely (TA 1988 ss.383 and 75).

Roll-over Relief

Roll-over relief means that tax on most business assets used in both corporate and unincorporated businesses can be deferred. The relief is an essential part of business planning and the difficult rules relating to its applicability should be studied whenever a disposal is in prospect (see chapter 19).

Although strictly a deferral, roll-over relief can in certain circumstances effectively operate as avoidance. Once a new asset has been genuinely used solely for business purposes, there is no claw-back of the relief if its business use ceases. Accordingly, it can be appropriated to investment. This is particularly so with land and buildings, where premises bought for the business can subsequently be vacated and let.

Individuals enjoy one particular advantage with roll-over relief, which is that migration does not occasion a claw-back of the relief. Accordingly, a disposal of the new asset subsequent to migration avoids the rolled-over as well as any subsequent gain. It is necessary for the individual to cease trading in the UK before migrating, since otherwise the gain may be taxed as a branch or agency gain (see p 134). But it is not necessary for the individual to acquire the new asset before migration. Roll-over relief is fully available if the old asset is disposed of in a UK trade which ceases before migration, and the new asset is acquired in a foreign trade thereafter. This is particularly valuable for sole traders who, for commercial reasons, need to sell their business before migration and so cannot avoid CGT on that sale by first becoming non-resident.

This opportunity to use roll-over for avoidance is not available to companies. When a company migrates, gains on prior disposals cannot be rolled forward (see p 135). At one time it was possible to get round this difficulty by continuing a branch or agency trade in the UK for a while, but this was blocked in 1989 (see p 134).

1982 rebasing has opened up one further planning possibility with roll-over relief. Under FA 1988 Sch 9, the rolled-over gain is reduced by half where the old asset was disposed of before 6 April 1988, regardless of when the old asset is acquired. Accordingly, those who disposed of business assets in the two years or so prior to 6 April 1988 may still be able to halve the gain by acquiring a new asset to roll into.

The decision to incorporate

One of the most important decisions in the early years of a business is the decision as to whether it should be incorporated. This decision is largely governed by commercial factors such as the protection of limited liability. But tax is always material, and, so far as tax is concerned, the balance now lies decisively with remaining unincorporated.

Sole traders and partners pay tax on profits at the maximum rate of 40 per cent, and, once that tax is paid, the profits are immediately at the disposal of the proprietors. The only corporate situation to match this is the small company paying out its profits as dividend. That apart, companies always occasion higher tax. Companies paying the main rate of corporation tax involve an extra 8 per cent tax on distributed profits and if the profits are not distributed, CGT has to be faced by the shareholders on a sale or liquidation.

Corporate or individual ownership

If a business does have to be incorporated, the question arises of whether the capital assets should be owned by the company or by the shareholders individually. Now that corporate gains are fully assimilated with income profits, this is largely governed by the same considerations as apply in deciding whether the business should be incorporated at all.

If the assets are kept outside the company, any disposal occasions only one lot of tax before the proceeds are at the disposal of the shareholders. Furthermore all the sheltering opportunities open to individuals are available. If the assets are in the company, any gain is liable to corporation tax. Should the net gain be distributed, the ACT credit is given against the mainstream tax (see p 165). But that only results in the same tax as directly owned assets bear if the company is a small company, for otherwise the ACT credit is not exhaustive (see p 166). Should the gain be retained by the company it will effectively attract the second charge to CGT on any sale or liquidation.

Keeping assets outside the company does involve other tax considerations. In particular, retirement relief is not available to the extent that the company pays rent for the asset (see p 100), and the rate of inheritance tax business property relief is 30 rather than 50 per cent (IHTA 1984 s.105(1)(d)). But these points do not outweigh the other drawbacks of corporate ownership, and it is to be noted that the most important relief of all, roll-over relief, can be claimed in respect of assets used by a family company but owned by shareholders (see p 118).

Methods of incorporation

The incorporation of an existing business has CGT consequences if assets are transferred to the new company. It might be thought that if the advice just given was followed, no assets would need to be transferred. But this ignores the fact that commercial considerations may require the transfer of assets and it should also be remembered that goodwill may attach to the business. Goodwill is as much an asset as any other, and inevitably incorporation will see it transferred to the company.

One method of incorporation is to rely on the CGT relief specifically applicable on incorporation, whereby any gain on the assets transferred is rolled into the company shares (see p 120). But this relief only applies where all the assets are transferred to the company and so it is inappropriate if assets are being kept out of the company. It can also have stamp duty and income costs.

If the only asset going into the company is goodwill, a better solution is to sell the trading stock etc at cost, and then claim hold-over relief in respect of any gain on the goodwill (see p 108). This solution is unsatisfactory if assets other than goodwill are being transferred, for the element of gift means that the held-over gain is potentially taxable both when the company disposes of the assets and when the shareholder sells the shares.

Groups

Once a company is formed and established, it may wish to divide up its business or start new businesses. In these circumstances the question arises of whether all the business activities should be carried on by the one company or whether the different activities should be transferred to specially formed subsidiaries.

As with the basic decision to incorporate, the decision to form subsidiaries and so create a group is largely governed by commercial considerations. But insofar as CGT is relevant, groups may be regarded as unsatisfactory, for they involve the creation of new assets, namely the shares in the subsidiaries, and new entities, namely the subsidiaries themselves. It may be possible to prevent unnecessary gains accruing as a result, but at the very least, time-consuming and expensive planning can be involved.

A particular difficulty arises when a subsidiary is sold or liquidated, for any uplift in the value of the shares is a chargeable gain. This difficulty is sometimes avoided by causing the subsidiary to pay a dividend first, but, if this is done the value shifting rules relating to groups must be watched (see p 68).

Disposals within a group are treated as no gain/no loss disposals, and so in this respect groups carry little disadvantage (see p 66). But groups are not treated as one in offsetting losses, and so the gains of company A are not relieved by the losses of company B. This difficulty is overcome in practice by routing disposals through group members with losses, but that can cause theoretical problems with the *Ramsay* principle, and real ones with roll-over relief (see pp 67 and 119).

Business planning

Mergers

Mergers have always been favourably treated by the tax code. CGT is no exception, and there is currently one well-recognised route whereby CGT on a merger may be deferred, namely the share-for-share exchange (see p 126). The relief for exchanges is available both where one company acquires the other and where both the companies being merged are acquired by a third specially formed for the purpose.

The relief is subject to a motive test, but a clearance procedure exists. Clearance should be applied for in all cases, and the application should normally be coupled with an application for income tax clearance under TA 1988 s.707.

Splits and demergers

Splitting a company or a group of companies is an exercise of great difficulty, for whereas mergers are favourably treated by the tax legislation, the same is not true of demergers. Splits, however, are frequently necessary in practice, either because the shareholders want to separate out several businesses, or because they have fallen out and different parties want to own different parts of the undertaking separately. CGT is by no means the only tax which has to be considered on a split, but often it is the most important.

Whenever a split is being contemplated, the first question to be asked is whether one or other part of the undertaking is really worth much. If its value is nominal it can simply be bought out by the shareholders who want it. Self evidently no CGT will be payable, and tax-planning will revolve round the consequences of a trading cessation, and the carry-forward of any unutilised losses.

Where both parts of the undertaking are valuable, the relief which normally comes to mind is the specific relief for demergers (see p 129). Unfortunately this is more useful in theory than in practice, for it is hedged about with restrictions. It only applies where both parts of the undertaking are and continue trading, and it is subject to a motive test. Furthermore, the relief does not in law confer CGT relief on the company effecting the distribution, and reliance has accordingly to be placed on concessionary treatment in SP 5/85.

An alternate way of proceeding is to achieve the split by a liquidation agreement under s.110 of the Insolvency Act 1986. Here, the liquidator is authorised to distribute the different parts of the business or different subsidiaries to the shareholders in satisfaction of their rights in the liquidation. The idea of proceeding in this way is that the exercise will be treated as a reconstruction, thereby enabling both the shareholders' and the corporate gains to be deferred (see p 127). But a split is not a reconstruction in law (see p 128), and so once again reliance has to be placed on the concessionary treatment in SP 5/85.

A final possibility is simply to distribute one of the businesses being split. If all the shareholders are retaining both businesses, the distribution can be by dividend in specie. If this is not the case, the distribution should be in consideration of the company buying-in the shares of the shareholders concerned, the transaction being structured so as not to attract the income tax relief for the purchase of own shares (see p 167). Taking this route is prohibitively expensive if the distributing company does not have mainstream tax capacity to absorb the ACT, and, even if it does, the recipient shareholders face 20 per cent tax on the net dividend. But this may be an acceptable price to pay for certainty of tax treatment.

Parallel companies

The proprietors of a privately owned company need not carry on a new business venture through that company. It is open to them to form a new company and, if they do this, certain CGT advantages may be obtained.

First, it may be possible to put right previous errors in relation to the ownership of the original company's shares. When that company was formed, the proprietors may have retained all the shares themselves, and now any transfer of the shares to their children or to trusts may require planning to deal with gains which have already accrued. Shares in a new company will not present these difficulties and their ownership can be got right at the offset. Second, if the new company prospers and comes to be sold, any gain will be immediately at the disposal of the shareholders. Were the business in the original company, any gain would go into that company, and, as described above, further tax would have to be faced before it could reach the shareholders.

Parallel companies do carry certain disadvantages. In particular, the lack of a group structure means that assets cannot be transferred from one company to another on a no gain/no loss basis, and the various other reliefs applicable to groups are lost. A further problem arises if the shareholders fall out and

Business planning

wish to divide up their businesses. With parallel companies, there is really no alternative to simply swapping shares, a transaction not covered by any of the available CGT reliefs.

Selling an unincorporated business

If a substantial CGT liability is in prospect on the sale of an unincorporated business, the tax may be avoided by the taxpayer becoming non-resident before the disposal (see p 149). The difficulty here is that non-residents who trade in the UK through a branch or agency remain liable to CGT, so it is necessary to achieve a cessation before becoming non-resident. At one time the Revenue did not tax branch or agency gains accruing after departure but in the same year, but this is no longer so (ESC D2, as revised 6 April 1989).

Taxpayers who cannot achieve a cessation before departure or are uneasy about relying on Revenue practice can consider the alternate course of transferring the business to a company, and then selling the shares in the company in the year of assessment following departure. If this is done, the gain on the assets is rolled into the shares, where it is tax-free once the taxpayer is non-resident (see p 120).

For the more normal taxpayer who is not contemplating migration, the relief to consider is retirement relief. This is material if the taxpayer is over 60 or retiring through ill-health, and is of increasing value now that the relief is partially available on gains between £125,000 and £500,000 (see chapter 16).

Selling a company

The sale of a company involves different considerations to the sale of an unincorporated business, for, so long as the purchaser is another company, one well recognised means of deferral is available. This is the share-for-share exchange, whereby the acquiring company issues shares to the vendor instead of cash. Indeed, the purchaser need not dilute its equity by issuing shares, for loan notes or loan stock will suffice (see p 127).

The opportunities opened up by this deferral are twofold. First the taxpayer may defer the realisation of the gain until he dies, or, if he is contemplating retirement abroad, until he becomes non-resident. Second, he can realise the gain in stages, taking advantage of each year's annual exemption and any losses which he may then have available.

Selling a company

The relief is subject to a motive test, but in practice this is only invoked in cases of undue artificiality, as where the purchaser issues loan-stock with a very short life. Advance clearance should however always be applied for. At one time, the relief could not apply to any earn-out element in the consideration, but now, if certain conditions are satisfied, in practice it can (see p 127).

If the vendor wishes to recieve cash rather than paper, he will normally have to accept some tax. But two factors may enable it to be mitigated.

First, it may be appropriate to declare a substantial dividend. This will be worth considering if the company has unutilised corporation tax capacity against which to set the ACT on the dividend, for then the sole tax cost will be the higher-rate tax payable by the shareholder. That tax cost works out at 20 per cent of the net dividend, half the CGT which would be payable if the amount distributed was realised as capital gain. It is necessary for the company to have distributable reserves and the application of the *Ramsay* principle must be considered. But the latter will not be material so long as the dividend is paid before negotiations for the sale begin or even, it seems, before they are concluded (*Craven v White* [1988] STC 476).

The second factor is retirement relief. This is as valuable on selling a company as on selling an unincorporated business. One important trap to remember is that the vendor must be a director until on or after the date of disposal. If he is not, one of the basic conditions for the applicability of the relief is lost.

Chapter 27

Capital and income

Introduction

The rates of tax on capital and income are now the same. This was brought about in 1987 for companies and in 1988 for individuals and trusts (see chapters 10-12)

Prior to this change, and the associated reductions in income tax rates, it was always more attractive to receive capital gains rather than income. For individuals, the comparison was between the flat 30 per cent tax on gains and the top rate of 60 per cent on income. For discretionary and accumulation trusts, the comparison was between rates of 30 and 45 per cent. With companies, gains were reduced by a specified fraction, most recently one seventh, before being included in profits.

Now that income and gains bear the same burden of tax, it matters much less whether a gain is capital or income. Indeed, the question may be asked of whether the distinction matters at all. There is no easy answer to this question, and each situation turns on its own facts. In this final chapter, four situations which frequently arise in practice are looked at.

Trading and investment

It is often difficult to tell whether the profit from an isolated transaction is a trading profit or an investment gain. The problem most frequently arises with land, and the issue turns on whether or not the taxpayer acquired the land with a view to resale (*Simmons v IRC* [1980] STC 350). Strictly, the taxpayer's intention is a matter of objective evidence. But, in practice, what he says his intention was, and the way in which he structures the transaction, carry great weight. Accordingly, the question which arises is whether in these respects he should seek to establish a trading intention or an investment intention.

Dividends and capital gains

In computational terms, the main advantages of a gain being an investment gain are the availability of the indexation allowance and the basic annual exemption. But indexation is of little use to assets with a low or nominal base cost, and the annual exemption is not available to companies.

There are some advantages in a gain being a trading profit, for all proper trading deductions are available. The CGT base value, by contrast, can only include the acquisition cost and enhancement expenditure reflected in the state or nature of the asset (see chapter 6). A CGT deduction for interest is never permitted to individuals, and it is only allowed to companies indirectly as a charge on income.

For individuals, a trading profit may have the further advantage of being easier to shelter. Individuals cannot shelter realised capital gains, save by offset against allowable capital losses of the same or a preceding year (see p 5). Trading profits, by contrast are available for general set-off and in particular may be relieved by losses from other trades and by such shelters as the Business Expansion Scheme and commercial buildings in enterprise zones.

A tentative overall conclusion is that profits generated on a rapid resale are better treated as trading, for any CGT indexation allowance will be small and unlikely to exceed the proper trading deductions. But if the asset is being retained for years rather than months, the indexation allowance is more valuable, particularly at a time of inflation and little real growth in asset values. In these circumstances an investment gain is more attractive. Since the investment intention is more likely to be established the longer an assset is held, what suits the taxpayer will thus accord with what he is likely to be able to prove.

Dividends and capital gains

The ever-present question for shareholders in private trading companies is whether they should take the company's profit in dividend or leave them in the company for realisation on an eventual sale or liquidation. Until 1988 retention was the better course, and indeed the prime objective of most entrepreneurs was to retain profits and build a company for sale or flotation. In purely computational terms, there is no doubt that the changes in tax rates have turned this on its head and now the payment of dividends is more attractive than retention.

Where the company is paying the main rate of corporation tax, total tax on dividends is 48 per cent. This is computed as follows:

Capital and income

Profit		100
Corporation tax		35
Dividend	65	
ACT	21.66	
Grossed up	86.66	
Higher rate tax on grossed up dividend	13	13
Total tax		48

These figures contrast with the position if profits are left in the company until a sale or liquidation. Assuming the gain then accruing is liable to CGT the total tax is as follows:

Profit		100
Corporation tax		35
Retained profit	65	
CGT thereon	26	26
Total tax		61

Dividends are still more attractive if the company is paying the small companies rate of corporation tax, for here the ACT set-off against mainstream tax is complete. Total tax on dividends is therefore 40 per cent—25 per cent borne by the company and 15 per cent by the shareholder. This contrasts as follows with the position if profits are retained.

Profit		100
Corporation tax		25
Retained profit	75	
CGT thereon (assuming it is fully reflected in the value of the shares)	30	30
Total tax		55

In most cases, the difference in total tax which these figures disclose indicates dividends should be paid. However, there are disadvantages, not least that the company may need the profits to fund expansion. In theory, the shareholders could loan back the dividends, but they will still have been diminished by higher-rate tax. Another point is that regular payment of dividends could increase the value of minority holdings. This does not matter if the company is simply going to be sold or liquidated, but IHT or CGT problems could arise in the event of a shareholder dying or giving his shares away.

A further factor to stress is that the higher-rate tax charge on dividends is immediate, whereas the CGT on any sale or liquidation is deferred. Furthermore, circumstances exist in which it would be wholly avoided, as where the shareholder dies or becomes non-resident. The charge may also be reduced by indexation, but only if the shares have a high base cost and the company does not own substantial assets whose rising values themselves cause the value of the company to keep pace with inflation.

Purchase of own shares

Section 162 of the Companies Act 1985 makes it possible for a company to purchase its own shares. In the absence of special provision, such a purchase is a distribution, resulting in an ACT liability for the company and a higher-rate tax liability for the shareholder. Until 1982 this made the tax cost of a purchase of own shares prohibitive, and for that reason provisions were introduced preventing certain purchases of own shares from being distributions (TA 1988 s.219).

To come within these provisions the company must be an unquoted trading company and the purchase must be effected for the benefit of its trade rather than effected for tax avoidance reasons. A whole series of other conditions must also be satisfied and, if the relief applies, the purchase is not taxed as a distribution but any gain realised by the shareholder is liable to CGT. A clearance procedure exists and, uniquely, the taxpayer can require the Revenue either to say that the conditions for the relief are satisfied, or that they are not (TA 1988 s.225).

Until 1988, the tax cost meant that a purchase which did not satisfy the conditions for relief was rarely worthwhile. Now, however, this is not so, and indeed there are cases where the clearance procedure needs to be used to ensure that the so called relief does *not* apply.

In deciding whether to seek the relief, the comparison which has to be made is between the CGT cost with the relief and the ACT and income tax cost without. There are two key factors in making this comparison, namely the base value of the shares and the extent to which the company has spare corporation tax capacity to offset the ACT. Surplus ACT may be offset against spare mainstream tax capacity for the preceding six accounting periods, but otherwise can only be carried forward (TA 1988 s.239).

If the company does have corporation tax capacity in the current or preceding accounting periods, the sole tax cost of a share purchase which does not attract the relief is higher-rate tax equal to 15 per cent of the grossed-up price, which works out as 20 per cent of the actual price. This tax cost will be less than that of a purchase within the relief, provided the indexed base cost of the shares equals or exceeds half the proceeds. If, as is commonly

Capital and income

the case, it is less, CGT on a purchase within the relief will be more than income tax on one outside it, and the purchase should be structured accordingly.

Matters become more difficult if the ACT on any purchase which does not attract the relief is not fully covered by spare mainstream tax capacity. Here the ACT which is unable to be offset will represent an extra cost, only able to be relieved in future accounting periods if profits are made and retained. In these circumstances a purchase qualifying for the relief is distinctly attractive and is only to be eschewed if the CGT base value of the shares really is very low indeed.

Share option and profit-sharing schemes

Where an employee of a company exercises an option to acquire shares in the company, the basic rule is that the difference between the price he pays and the value of the shares is taxable under Schedule E (TA 1988 s.135). So too, shares advanced to an employee under an employee share trust are taxable as an emolument (*Brumby v Milner* [1976] STC 534, HL). In both cases these consequences are avoided if a long list of conditions set out in TA 1988 Sch 9 are satisfied. Option schemes satisfying these conditions are known as approved share option schemes and trusts as approved profit-sharing schemes. The question which arises is whether, given the assimilation of the rates of tax on income and gains, it is worth satisfying the conditions.

If a share option scheme is an approved scheme, tax is not charged on the exercise of the option, but the CGT base cost of the shares is what the employee in fact pays rather than market value (TA 1988 s.188(3)(b)). This means that when the shares are sold, the gain for CGT purposes is the undervalue plus any subsequent gain and the indexation allowance is based on the low actual acquisition cost. If the scheme is unapproved, income tax is payable on the undervalue immediately the option is exercised, but the CGT base cost and indexation are based on the full value of the shares (CGTA 1979 s.32A).

Where, as is commonly the case, the employee disposes of the shares immediately after he exercises the option, there is little to choose between approved and unapproved schemes, and indeed, because an income tax charge can be offset by shelters such as BES shares, an unapproved scheme may be preferable. But if the employee retains the shares, an approved scheme is more attractive, for the CGT is deferred and may indeed never be paid if the employee dies or becomes non-resident. Since an

Share option and profit-sharing schemes

approved scheme avoids the immediate tax charge, it is also normally to be recommended where, when the scheme is set up, it is unclear whether the employees will immediately sell or retain the shares.

With employee share trusts, the tax position is much more clear-cut. If the trust is an approved profit-sharing scheme, an appropriation of shares within eighteen months of acquisition is not an emolument, and it is treated as an exempt market-value disposal for CGT purposes (CGTA 1979 s.144A). If the trust is unapproved, the appropriation is liable to Schedule E in the hands of the employee, and CGT is payable on any uplift in the value of the shares. This CGT will normally be able to be deferred by a hold-over relief election (see p 108), but the held-over gain will be potentially taxable and, if it is taxed, it will have attracted both income tax and CGT.

The disadvantage with approved profit-sharing schemes is that annual appropriations are restricted to 10 per cent of salary, or £6,000, whichever is less. Furthermore, all employees have to be beneficiaries under the trust. For this reason, approved schemes are inappropriate for large-scale rewards to key personnel.

Index

1982 rebasing
  basic rule, 5
  disposals
    no gain/no loss 44–45
  election, 41
    taxpayers, 43–44
  exclusions, 41–43
  general, 40
  groups and, 67–68
  held-over and rolled-over gains, 45–47
  replacement of business assets and, 118
  roll-over relief, 123
Absence
  private residence, from, 80–82
Accomodation
  job-related, 80–81
  private residence. See PRIVATE RESIDENCE
Acquisition cost
  allowable expenditure, 28–29
Advance corporation tax (ACT)
  mainstream corporation tax, set against, 64
Advertising
  incidental costs, 30
Agency
  non-resident company trading through, 134
Agricultural property
  hold-over relief, 109
Allowable expenditure. See EXPENDITURE
Allowance
  capital. See CAPITAL ALLOWANCE
  indexation. See INDEXATION
Amalgamation. See COMPANY
Annual exemption
  individual entitled to, 59–60
  separation, effect to, 61

Annual exemption – *continued*
  trustees, 72–73
Anti-avoidable. See AVOIDANCE
Apportionment
  costs of, 28
  non-resident company, 139–140
Assets
  1982 rebasing, 5
  business
    gifts of, 107–108
    replacement of. See ROLL-OVER RELIEF
    settled, 108–109
  capital sum derived from, 12–14
  chargeable business, retirement relief, 97
  construction of term, 6–7
  death, on. See DEATH
  destroyed, 14, 122–123
  disposal of. See DISPOSAL
  dissipation of, 14
  exempt, 9
  extinction of, 14
  general, 6
  held on 31 March 1982, 51–52
  indexation. See INDEXATION
  interests in, 7
  limitation on term, 7
  liquidator, vested in, 65
  lost, 14, 122–123
  market value. See MARKET VALUE
  negligible value, of, 14
  roll-over relief. See ROLL-OVER RELIEF
  showing a gain, 152–153
  spatial difficulties, 8
  specific, 6–7
  spreading around the family, 154
  temporal difficulties, 8
  unidentifiable, 7–8
  unindexed, 55

Index

Assets – *continued*
  valueless, 14–15
  wasting. *See* WASTING ASSETS
Avoidance
  group of companies, by, 61
  private residence exemption, 85

Bank accounts
  foreign currency, 88
Base date
  1965, 40, 43
Bonds
  qualifying corporate, 9, 86–87
  1982, 5, 40–41
Branch
  non-resident company trading through, 134–135
Business
  Expansion Scheme, (BES)
    share, exemption for, 89–90
    shares, 168
      exempt assets as, 9
    tax planing, 153
  planning
    capital assets
      corporate ownership, 158
      individual ownership, 158
    decision to incorporate, 157–158
    demergers, 160–161
    general, 156
    groups, 159–160
    incorporation, methods of, 158–159
    mergers, 160
    parallel companies, 161–162
    roll-over relief, 156–157
    sale of company, 162–163
    splitting a company, 160–161
    unincorporated business, sale of, 162
  private residence, use of, 83
  replacement of assets. *See* ROLL-OVER RELIEF
  retirement relief. *See* RETIREMENT RELIEF
  transfer to company, roll-over relief, 120–121
  unincorporated, 97–98

Capital
  asset, sum derived from, 12–14
  payment, non-resident trust, 144–145
  tax planning. *See* PLANNING

Capital allowance
  allowable expenditure, 30–31
  wasting assets qualifying for, 34
Caravan
  exemption, 79
Cars
  exempt assets, 9
Chargeable entities
  company. *See* COMPANY
  individual. *See* INDIVIDUAL
  settlement. *See* SETTLED PROPERTY
  trust. *See* TRUST
Chargeable gains. *See* GAINS
Chattels. *See* EXEMPT CHATTELS
Claw-back
  hold-over relief, 111–112
Commodities
  unindentifiable assets, as, 7
Company
  advance corporation tax, 64–65
  allowable losses, 58
  amalgamation,
    general, 127–128
    motive test, 158–159
    no gain/no loss disposals, 44
    relief, 127–128
  chargeable gains, 3, 64
  connections, 19–20
  corporation tax, liability to, 64
  demerger, 129, 160–161
  double taxation, 65–66
  dual resident, 138
  family, roll-over relief, 118
  family trading, shares in, retirement relief, 98–99
  general, 64
  groups
    1982 rebasing and, 67–68
    indexation and, 68
    intra group disposals, 66–67
    non-resident, 141
    roll-over relief, 118–119
    splitting of, 160–161
    tax planning, 159
    treatment for CGT purposes, 66
  hold-over relief, 108
  liquidation, 65
  mergers, 160
  non-resident. *See* NON-RESIDENT
  parallel, 161–162
  reconstruction,
    general, 124, 127–128
    motive test, 128–129
    no gain/no loss disposals, 44

Index

Company - *continued*
  reconstruction - *continued*
    relief, 127–128
    temporal difficulties, 8
  reorganistion, 8
  residence, 133–134
  sale of, 162–163
  small, 64–65
  splitting a, 160–161
  tax planning, 156
  transfer of business to, roll-over relief, 120–121
  unit trust, 69. *See also* SHARES
Compensation
  statutory rights to, not asset, 7
  roll-over relief, 121–122
Computation
  allowable expenditure. *See* EXPENDITURE
  allowable losses, 4–5
  chargeable gains, 3–4
  consideration. *See* CONSIDERATION
  general, 3
  identification. *See* IDENTIFICATION
  pooling. *See* POOLING
Connected persons
  categories of, 18
  companies, 18–19
  persons not connected, 19
  transaction between, 18
Connections
  company, 19–20
Consideration
  amount of, 23–24
  contingent, 25–26
  deferred, 25
  general, 23
  income receipts, 24–25
  value shifting, 24
Corporation tax
  advance, 64–65
  double taxation, 65–66
  liability for, 64
Costs
  acquisition, 28–29
  incidental, 29–30
Currency. *See* FOREIGN CURRENCY

Damages
  exempt intangible as, 88–89
Death
  allowable losses, 101
  deed of variation, 102–103
  deemed reaquisition, 101

Death - *continued*
  legatees, 102
  personal representatives, 101–102
  tax planning, 155
Debts
  asset, designation as, 6
  exemption, 87
Decorations
  exemption, 93
Deed of variation
  death, on, 102–103
Deferral
  hold-over relief. *See* HOLD-OVER RELIEF
  replacement of business assets. *See* ROLL-OVER RELIEF
Dependent relative
  private residence exemption, 84
Disposal
  actual, 10–11, 72
  associated, 99–100
  capital sum derived from asset, 12–14
  consideration received on. *See* CONSIDERATION
  deemed, 12–14, 72
  deferrals, 15–16
  destruction of asset, 14
  dissipation of asset, 14
  employee, 100
  exempt, 15–16
  extinction of asset, 14
  gain accrues on, 6
  intra group, 66–67
  liquidator, by, 59
  loss accrues on, 6
  lost asset, 14–15
  no loss/no gain, 15, 44–45
  part. *see* PART DISPOSAL
  retirement relief. *See* RETIREMENT RELIEF
  time of, 11
  trustee, 100
  valueles asset, 14–15
  value shifting, 14
Dividends
  tax planning, 165–167
Divorce
  relief for disposal between spouses, loss of, 61
Double taxation
  company, 65–66
  non-resident company, 141
  territorial limits, 137–138

173

Index

Double taxation – *continued*
  unit limits, 69
Dual resident
  territorial limits, 138

Easement
  asset, as, 7
Election
  1982 rebasing, 41
Employee
  disposal by, retirement relief, 100
Enhancement expenditure
  forms of, 27
  improvements, 27
  preservation, 27
Exempt chattels
  decorations, 93
  foreign currency, 93–94
  medals, 93
  not exceeding £6,000 in value, 92–93
  vehicle, 93
  wasting assets, 93
  worth less than £6,000, 9
Exempt intangibles
  BES shares, 89–90
  damages, 88–89
  debts, 87
  foreign currency bank accounts, 88
  gilts, 86
  personal equity plans, 90–91
  qualifying corporate bonds, 86–87
Exemption
  annual. *See* ANNUAL EXEMPTION
  chattel. *See* EXEMPT CHATTELS
  death. *See* DEATH
  intangibles. *See* EXEMPT INTANGIBLES
  private residence. *See* PRIVATE RESIDENCE
  retirement relief. *See* RETIREMENT RELIEF
Expenditure
  allowable,
    acquisition cost, 28–29
    capital allowances, 30–31
    enhancement expenditure, 29
    general, 28
    incidental costs, 29–30
    income expenditure, 30
    leases, 33–34
    part disposals, 31
    renewals allowances, 30–31
    wasting assets, 32–33

Expenditure – *continued*
  income, 30

Family
  spreading assets around the, 154
Family trading company
  shares in, retirement relief, 98–99
Foreign currency
  asset, designation as, 6
  bank accounts, 88
  exempt asset, 9
  exemption, 93–94
Freehold land
  asset, as, 7

Gains
  1982 rebasing, 5
  assets showing, 152–153
  attribution of,
    to settlor, 73–74
  capital
    tax planning, 165–167
  chargeables
    allowable losses set against, 4–5
    company, of, 3, 64
    computation, 3–4
    trading stock giving rise to, 25
  disposal of asset, requirement of, 6
  indexation. *See* INDEXATION
  postponed, 47–48
  sheltering substantial, 149–150
  term not defined, 3, 4
Garden
  exempt asset, 9
  private residence exemption
    qualification for, 83
Gifts
  business assets of, 107–108
  death on, 155
  hold-over relief, 155
Gilts
  exemptions, 86
  relevant securities as, 39
Grounds
  private residence exemption,
    qualification for, 83
Groups. *See* COMPANY

Hold-over gains
  1982 rebasing and, 45–47
Hold-over relief
  agricultural property, 109
  claw-back, 111–112
  company, 112

Index

Hold-over relief - *continued*
  dual residents and, 138
  general, 107
  gifts of business assets, 107-108
  individual, 111
  inheritance tax, 112
  operation of, 110-111
  payment of tax by instalments, 112
  settled business assets, 108-109
  settlement, 111
  tax planning, 154-155
  when applicable, 16

House. *See* PRIVATE RESIDENCE
Houseboat
  exemption, 79
Husband. *See* SPOUSES

Identification
  1982 rules, 36-37
  general, 35
  pooling and, 35-39
  unidentifiable assets, solution to problem of, 8, 35
Improvements
  enhancement expenditure, 29
Income
  disallowed expenditure, 30
  receipts, exclusion of, 5, 24-25
  tax planning. *See* TAX PLANNING
Income tax
  disallowed expenditure, 5
Incorporeal property
  asset, designation as, 6
Indexation
  allowance,
    application of, 49
    calculation, 50-51
  assets, 68
  assets held on 31 March 1982, 51-52
  general, 49
  groups and, 68
  parallel pooling, 53-55
  special situations, 52
  unindexed assets, 55
Individual
  annual exemption, 59-60
  connected person, 18
  divorce, 61-62
  hold-over relief, 109
  liability to tax, 3, 59
  migration, 135
  not-connected, 19
  partner. *See* PARTNER

Individual - *continued*
  rates of tax, 60
  residence, 133
  separation, 61-62
  spouses,
    1988-9, 61
    1989-90, 61
    separate taxation, 60-61
Inheritance tax
  hold-over relief, 109
Intangibles *see* EXEMPT INTANGIBLES
Interest
  asset in, 7
  beneficial, 74-75, 146
    exempt asset, 9
Investment
  capital and income, 164-165
  tax planning,
  trading and, 164-165

Land
  compulsory purchae, roll-over relief, 121-122
  freehold, as asset, 7
  allowable expenditure, 33-34
  asset, as, 7
  premium as consideration for part disposal, 26-27
  wasting asset, as, 9, 33
Legatee
  personal representative, disposal by, 102
Letting
  private residence, 82
Liquidation
  assets vetted in liquidator, 65
  disposals, 65
  shareholder, position of, 65
Losses
  allowable,
    company of, 64
    deceased, accruing to, 101
  disposal of asset, requirement of, 6
  indexation. *See* INDEXATION

Machinery
  wasting asset, as, 8
Market value
  connected persons, 18
  determining, 17-18
  substitution of, 17
Medals
  exemption, 93

175

Index

Migration
  company, of, 135
  individual, of, 135
  settlement, of, 145
Money
  consideration, 23
Motive test
  amalgamation, 128
  reconstruction, 128
  share for share exchange, 128

New holdings
  assets pooled as, 37
Non-resident
  company,
    agency in UK, trading through, 134–135
    apportionment, 139
    branch in UK trading through, 134–135
    double taxations, 141
    general, 139
    groups, 141
    relief, 140
    trustee shareholders, 141
Non-resident trust
  beneficial interests, 146
  capital payments, 144–145
  gains, attribution of, 142–143
  general, 142
  initial, 151–152
  migration, 145
  territorial limits, 143–144
  transfer or settled property, 145

Option
  asset, as, 6, 7
  monies as consideration, 27
  wasting asset, as, 8

Part disposal
  allowable expenditure, 31
  when occuring, 11
Partner
  connected person, 18
  liability to tax, 62–63
  not connected, 19
Payment of tax by instalments
  hold-over relief, 112
Personal Equity Plans (PCPs)
  exemption, 90–91
  investments in a, exempt asset, 9
  tax planning, 153, 154

Personal planning. *See* TAX PLANNING
Personal representative
  death and, 101–102
  legateee, disposal to, 102
Planning. *See* TAX PLANNING
Plant
  wasting asset, as, 8
Pooling
  1982, holdings, 38
  abolition of, 36
  application of, 36
  general, 35
  identification and, 35–39
  new holdings, 37
  reintroduction, 36–37
  relevant securities, 38–39
  unidentifiable assets, solution to problem of, 7, 35
Portfolio investor
  tax planning, 153–154
Postponed gains. *See* GAINS
Preservation
  enhancement expenditure, 29
Private residence
  anti-avoidance, 85
  business use, 83
  dependent relatives, 84
  exemption, 79
  garden, 83
  grounds, 83
  lettings, 82
  periods of absence, 80–82
  settled property, 83–84
  staff accomodation, 79
  two or more, 79–80
Professional charges
  incidental costs, as, 30
Profit-sharing schemes
  tax planning, 168–169
Property
  incorporeal, designation as asset, 6
  private residence. *See* PRIVATE RESIDENCE
  taxpayer, created by, designation as asset, 6

Qualifying corporate bonds
  exempt asset, 9, 86–87
  relevant securities as, 39

Rates of tax
  capital and income, 164
  individual, 60
  trust, 73

176

Index

Reconstruction. *See* COMPANY
Relative. *See* DEPENDANT RELATIVE
Relief
  amalgamation. *See* COMPANY
  double taxation. *See* DOUBLE
    TAXATION
  hold-over. *See* HOLD-OVER RELIEF
  non-resident company, 140
  reconstruction. *See* COMPANY
  re-organisation. *See* SHARES
  retirement. *See* RETIREMENT RELIEF
  roll-over. *See* ROLL-OVER RELIEF
  share for share exchange. *See*
    SHARES
Remittance
  basis, 136
  delayed, 136–137
Renewals allowance
  allowable expenditure, 30–31
Rent
  consideration, does not count as, 24
Reorganisation. *See* SHARES
Replacement of business assets. *See*
  ROLL-OVER RELIEF
Residence
  exempt assets, 9
  non-resident. *See* NON-RESIDENT
  territorial limits, 133–134. *See also*
    PRIVATE RESIDENCE
Retirement relief
  amount available for, 96–97
  availability, 95–96
  chargeable business assets, 97
  conditions for, 95
  disposal,
    associated, 99–100
    employee, 100
    qualifying, 95–96
    trustee, 100
  family trading company, shares in, 98–99
  general, 95
  qualifying period, 96
  unincorporated business, 97–98
Roll-over relief
  1982 rebasing and, 45–47, 118
  application of, 16
  assets,
    classes of, 114
    destroyed, 122–123
    lost, 122–123
    new, 115
    new depreciating, 117
    old, 115

Roll-over relief – *continued*
  business planning, 156–157
  compulsory purchase, 121–122
  dual residence, 138
  family company, 118
  groups, 118–119
  operation of, 116–117
  partial reinvestment, 117
  persons eligible, 113–114
  time limits, 116
  transfer of business to company, 120–121
  when applicable, 15, 113
Securities
  conversion of,
    general, 124
    meaning, 126
    relief, 124–125
  market value, 17–18
  relevant, 37, 38–39
  unidentifiable assets, as, 7
Securities. *See also* SHARES
Separation
  annual exemption, 61–62
Settled property
  hold-over relief, 108
  meaning, 70–71
  nominee property distinguished from, 70
  private residence exemption, 84
  transfer of, 145
  trustees, 71
  see also TRUST
Settlor
  attribution of gains to, 73–74
  connected person, 18
  not connected person, 19
Shareholders
  ever present question of, 165
  liquidation, position with regard to, 65
  trustee, non-resident company, 141
Shares
  assets, as, 7
  Business Expansion Scheme, exemption for, 89–90
  demerger, 129
  family trading company, in, retirement relief, 98–99
  market value, 18
  options
    tax planning, 168–169
  purchase of,
    tax planning, 167–168

177

Index

Shares - *continued*
  reorganisation,
    general, 124
    meaning, 125
    relief, 124-125
  share for share exchange,
    general, 124
    motive test, 128
    qualification for relief, 126-127
    relief, 124
  value shifting, 14
Small company
  rate of corporation tax, 64
Spouses
  1988-9, 61
  1989-90, 61
  divorce, 61
  no gain/no loss disposal, 44
  separate taxation, 60-61
  separation, 61-62
Staff
  accommodation for, 79

Tax planning
  business. *see* BUSINESS
  company, 156
  dividends and capital gains, 165-167
  gifts
    death, and, 155
    hold-over relief, and, 155
  investment,
  long term, 150-151
  portfolio investors, 153-154
  profit-sharing schemes, 168-169
  purchase of own shares, 167-168
  recent reforms, impact of,
  resident trusts, initially, 151-152
  share option, 168-169
  sheltering substantial gains, 149
  spreading assets round the family, 154
  trading and investment, 164-165
Taxpayer
  property created by, designation as asset, 6
Territorial limits
  delayed remittances, 136-137
  double taxation relief, 137-138
  dual residents, 138
  general, 133
  migration, 135
  remittance basis, 136

Territorial limits - *continued*
  residence, 133-134
  UK branch or agency, 134-135
  see also NON-RESIDENT
Trading
  capital and income, 164-165
  investment and, 164-165
Trading stock
  chargeable gain, giving rise to, 25
Trust
  actual disposal, 72
  basic annual exemption, 72-73
  beneficial interests, 7, 74, 75
  deemed disposal, 72
  initial resident, 151-152
  liability to tax, 3
  migration, 135
  non-resident. *See* NON-RESIDENT
  rates of tax, 73
  tax planning, 152
Trustee
  disposal by, retirement relief, 100
  connected persons, 18
  not connected, 19
  settled property, of, 71
  shareholder, non-resident company, 139

Unit trust
  authorised, 69
  double taxation, 69

Valuation
  costs of, 30
Value shifting
  consideration, 24
  deemed disposal at market value, 14
Vehicle
  exemption, 93

Wasting assets
  allowable expenditure, 32-33
  capital allowances, qualifying for, 32
Wasting assets - *continued*
  exemption, 9, 93
  lease, 8, 33-34
  option, 8
  plant and machinery, 8
  predictable life, 8
Wife *See* SPOUSES